Project Manager

All you need to be a complete project manager from getting the interview to managing small Project

SAMUEL PETERS

CONTENTS

INTRODUCTION

If you are yearning to be a great and efficient project manager, and find necessary to equip yourself with project managerial qualities and tips, and learn everything on how to become an exceptional one, read this book of wisdom. With details and tips to make you successfully overwhelm that interview and win the job.

There are many opinions regarding the definition of a manager. You will develop your managerial style over the course of your career, no matter what age you are as you enter management.

The most important thing to recognize is that your role is not to order people around; your role is to work them toward becoming self-directed. Your boss will measure you on the performance of your direct reports. Therefore, everything you do need to be with their best performance in mind — no matter what kind of style you develop as a manager.

For now, focus on establishing a good basis of respect between you and your direct reports. This will involve setting standards, building trust and confidence, providing performance feedback, demonstrating motivation, being a good listener, adapting to change, and providing constant communication.

One of the best methods for accomplishing all these things is by managing a project.

Successful project management demands that you listen to your client and your stakeholders (the people who benefit from the outcome). You and your team will analyze and substantiate the need to create the product or service that the project will generate. You will plan every aspect of activity that needs to occur and set standards to ensure your plans are accurate. After you give feedback to your sponsor and make required adaptations to your plans, you will then execute the project. As it launches, you will implement control measures and provide feedback, again adapt if necessary, and keep your team motivated if things do not turn out exactly as you had planned. Finally, you will close the project and provide evaluations to your crew. Your boss will evaluate you based on the outcome; therefore, staying focused on your team's success is vital.

This book is meant for those people who are interested project management and want to become professional project managers. It is intended to help you succeed in both arenas by providing you with pitfalls to avoid, how to get that job with interview success, as well as tips for success. It will not only address on how to manage conflict, but it will also walk you through the qualities of a real project manager and describe how to execute the task of a project manager.

By learning this process, you will propel your managerial skill set to levels that some experienced managers do not possess. A lot of project managers today have worked their entire lives without ever doing a project and learning the

Need for careful planning, honest communication, and conscientious control.

Conversely, consider that you will need help from other people at times to find solutions for problems that are new to you but not to them. This book will show you how to seek for assistance from subject matter experts when necessary.

Management today includes duties such as staffing, recruiting, training, developing, and directing. It also requires the manager to keep abreast of vast technological changes and different work environments. Today, a manager may have direct reports who telecommute or who are located in a remote city. This manager needs to use technology to connect with such employees. Measurement tools and software are becoming increasingly important to today's manager for evaluating every employee's output evenly.

As a good and informed project manager, you will need to get to know your team members and always be thinking about developing each one toward his or her own potential. A big part of that process is to challenge them by delegating and establishing goals for them.

A good first step is to speak to each member one-on-one. Ask each one to define his or her role and responsibility. This helps you understand the team member's function and ensures that your understanding is the same as his or hers. Next, ask him or her to define the roles and responsibilities of each of the other team members. This exercise can be beneficial for several reasons. First, it lets you hear everyone's function several times and thereby educates you about what everyone does. But even more important, it quickly identifies someone who does not know what another does. This will allow you to spot areas where you can build teamwork simply by having one person assist another. It also provides the added benefit of cross-training people in your team.

You always take heed of ensuring there are no physical or policy restraints that would prohibit you from asking one employee to share in another's work.

Also during these initial conversations, be certain to express that you care about each person as well as the achievement of the goals of your organization. Express that you intend to delegate to help the team members advance their own skills. This conveys that you will be expecting them to show you what they can do. Encourage them to let you know when something is concerning them or preventing them from achieving their best. You should always keep these meetings brief, if I may suggest less than 20 minutes if possible. You want to set the example of being friendly but succinct.

Many project managers, especially those who are new to the job may find delegation difficult. They fear it shows they are incapable or unwilling to do their own work, or worse, that they expect their direct reports to do their job for them.

Delegation produces many benefits. Employees learn new skills and become more involved in the team goals. The company now has cross- trained people who can help when you need an emergency stand- in. This frees you up to work toward your own effectiveness and development.

There are a few rules to delegation. Never delegate personnel items, such as salary treatment, feedback, or appraisals. Do not delegate with an uneven hand. Be aware of people who are not ready or are already too busy, and do not let your people delegate to you. This can happen when they claim they are overburdened or uncomfortable with the skills required for a given job. Use those instances as opportunities to train them or pull in another team member to assist them.

Feedback to all your employees is critical to their success and yours. Indeed, you should establish quarterly goals for each person and review them as they go. Having an informal, quarterly review allows the employee the opportunity to correct items as needed or to give you feedback about why things are not progressing well. By the time he or she receives the annual review, there should be no surprises on it.

If an employee is not performing up to standards, you can try breaking down the goals into smaller segments. For instance, if someone has a goal of producing 40 widgets per month and is falling short, consider breaking it down into 10 widgets per week. Sometimes just reducing the quantity will work.

Other times, you will find yourself facing the disciplinary process.

Many companies have their own inner standards about how to treat someone who is performing substandard. The critical rule here is to never discipline the person in public. These conversations should be behind a closed door; otherwise, you risk disaster. In the worse case, the employee might seek litigation against you for personal angst; in the best-case scenario, your message might not be immediately discarded before the employee sulks away.

Becoming a prolific and professional project manager, you need to entail the following attributes and skills to be successful in your projects

CREATE TRUST

The project manager should actively work to create an atmosphere of trust within his team and beyond into the larger organization to the greatest extent possible.

Many organizations suffer from a dysfunctional work environment which is detrimental to the performance of individuals and to the success of the organization. These environments are characterized by a number of attributes, one being a feeling of low trust among individuals within the organization. Low trust environments tend to be highly political where individuals work to personal agendas, putting their own needs above those of the company and making decisions that are detrimental to the success of the organization. Individuals in these environments tend to hoard information and are reluctant to share knowledge with other team members or management leading to lower productivity and less than optimal performance.

An open-minded project manager can minimize the effects of a low trust environment by beginning with his team and building an environment of trust within the team. This is best accomplished by "walking the talk" or by always behaving ethically with integrity, by keeping commitments, by open communication and by practicing transparency.

HAVE THE INTEGRITY TO STAND UP FOR YOURSELF

By not standing up for yourself, you will likely lose the respect of your team, as well as that of management, making any reason you might have for not standing up invalid.

Remember to always stand up for yourself. The worst thing that can happen is that you will be fired, (you can't be shot), and you will almost always move on to a better, higher-paying opportunity. Also remember that there is nothing of value to be gained by not standing up, and very much to lose if you don't do the right thing. Stand up for yourself and be happy and successful.

WORK TO BECOME A SERVANT LEADER

The idea of the command and control style of leadership, where the project manager directs his team in all daily tasks and makes all important decisions (usually while sitting alone in his or her office), is an old school idea steeped in the old industrial age management paradigm. Thankfully, this paradigm is beginning to die away (granted the death will be slow and painful, but it will be sure) to be replaced by a new style that is better suited to people in our current workforce.

The newer approach is more that of a servant leader, where the project manager assumes the role of someone who supports the team and helps members move in desired directions. This ensures that members have everything needed to accomplish work, including help removing roadblocks to that work, when necessary.

Accept the idea that your team collectively knows more about the work of the project than you do, and is best served by support, help, and guidance, rather than control and direction. Stay focused on the big picture where your knowledge and experience can be used most effectively. Resist the urge to direct and control, but rather try to guide and support the work.

BE TRANSPARENT

Be as transparent as possible as a project manager. In other words, work to minimize the amount of confidential or protected information associated with your project. You will be much more powerful and will enjoy greater success and productivity with the help of your team which cannot be fully realized if information is hidden from them.

Team members should be involved in the decision-making process to the greatest extent possible, which means they will need access to as much information as possible in order to make a meaningful contribution. The reasoning behind decisions made outside the team should be fully explained to encourage an environment of openness and reinforce the idea that the team members are a valuable part of the system. The team should also be informed as to the political environment in the performing organization, as well as on the customer's side of the fence.

While some information will need to remain confidential, the project manager should carefully examine the need for confidentiality and weigh that against the potential detrimental effects creating that restricted information could have on the performance of the team.

BE A MULTIPLIER

Have you ever seen an individual who was a top performer in one group be transferred to another group only to become a mediocre performer, or vice versa? Many times our actions as leaders can have a diminishing effect on a team member's performance even though that is not our intent.

Behaviors that tend to diminish performance include hoarding resources and information, creating a tense work environment, keeping the focus on one's own knowledge, centralized decision making, and a tendency to personally solve the team's problems (micromanaging).

Behaviors that tend to "multiply" good performance include attracting and fully utilizing talented people, creating a work environment that requires people to do their best thinking and work, providing stretch opportunities, practicing team-centric decision making, and crediting the team for success.

Consciously strive to be a multiplier rather than a spoiler.

GET CERTIFIED

A formal project management training or certification is one of the crucial documents one should have to become a qualified project manager.

Project management is a difficult undertaking under the best of conditions, and unfortunately, most of us don't work under the best of conditions. If you attempt to manage a project without a solid understanding of fundamentals or of the "mechanics" of how projects work (if you do this, you'll get that) you are setting yourself up for failure.

Many organizations are beginning to realize the value of training and certification as evidenced by the increased number of project manager job postings where certification is required. Experience or on-the-job training is good; however, in many cases it is just reinforcing bad habits or incorrect ideas and without theory to balance experience this method of learning project management could actually be detrimental.

Certifications such as the Project Management Professional (PMP) from the Project Management Institute (PMI) require experience as well as classroom training to even sit for the exam. Holders of the PMP certification have demonstrated a solid understanding of project management fundamentals and are that much more valuable to organizations. Take the time to get certified and enjoy greater success and rewards in your project management career.

CHAPTER 1

PROJECT MANAGEMENT

WHAT IS PROJECT MANAGEMENT?

In business, people with creative minds are necessary to come up with new innovations towards improvement or development of a particular service.

As ideas are brought to management, these are studied and evaluated. If management feels that the idea can be worked out, then study of the proposal is undertaken. This idea becomes a project to be studied.

DIFFERENT DEFINITION OF PROJECT MANAGEMENT

It is a temporary undertaking performs for the purpose of creating an innovative product or service that in the end will benefit and give worth to a company or individual.

Project Management is the facility for an individual or company to organize and manage knowledge and resources in order to deliver the work required for a specific project.

Project management means organizing, running, and bringing a project to its conclusion.

Project management can also be defined as the process and techniques to follow when you are doing something you have never done before or trying to improve something you have done before. This project would have to be managed. This activity is called Project Management.

Our lives are made up of a variety of projects, and how we go about managing the chaos of change can make us successful in our business and our personal lives.

So, You Have a project to manage a project, you first need to understand what constitutes a project. It includes the following:

•Defining the goal of the project

•Determining the results you expect to be accomplished

•Working within a budget

•Setting up a schedule

•Selecting your team and establishing individual roles

•Making sure the tools and technology are in place

•Monitoring ongoing progress

•Maintaining team morale and Dealing with problems that arise

•Keeping stakeholders abreast of your progress

Bringing the project to completion

•Assessing what went right and what went wrong

Defining the goal of the project: To move out of one home and move into another.

•Determining the results you expect to be accomplished: Everything is in its place and accounted for in the new project which is planned for.

•Working within a budget: A certain amount of money is usually allocated for different types of resources such as moving supplies, required materials, and new items for the new project.

•Setting up a schedule: The move date is a fixed date. Time must be allotted prior to the move date to ensure that everything is packed and ready to take place within the time given. Time will be allotted to make the move as well as unpack everything. Even though the move is on a specific date, the schedule will account for time before and after the actual move date.

•Selecting your team: The team may include just you or a few well selected members to assist or a moving company. The size (and scope) of the move can determine the best makeup of teams.

•Establishing the roles of each individual: Who is in charge of coordinating the utilities? Who will stay with the movers? Each and every member of the team should be allocated to his or her suiting position in the project to ensure that everything runs smoothly and efficiently.

•Monitoring ongoing progress: Keep track of what is left to be done. Establish a checklist of companies to notify of the move and monitor how many are left. Establish targets for which next move will be taken up next.

•Dealing with problems that arise: you should equip yourself with all possible solutions to any arising matter at hand.

•Bringing the project to completion: The move occurs.

•Assessing what went right and what went wrong: As a project manager you should always come up with solutions for any problem which may arise. Not everything goes well as the project progresses, there are always challenges that may arise but, you should be well equipped with the know how to go through all the challenges. As project manager, you know what is expected of you.

PROJECT MANAGEMENT EXISTENCE

It requires the management with focus on details, quality, time and budget restraints. Its function is to monitor, control and plan projects.

In as much as a project is temporary, activities need to be performed and delivered under some constraints such as scope, time and cost.

1) The time constraint deals on the amount of time given for the project to complete.

2) The cost restraint deals on the amount allotted for the project.

3) The scope constraint deals on what should be done to come up with the project's end result.

Due to these constraints, a careful planning and analysis of the project should be given so as not to experience wastage on the resources that have already placed into the project.

Let a group handle your proposed innovations and create a project management to handle such.

PROJECT MANAGEMENT BASICS

This is definitely the book you need to take you all the way through all the necessities needed to make you a perfect project manager.

The job of a project manager is to plan and manage projects. Later chapters will cover the many advanced aspects of project management.

Before we dive into the many facets of planning and managing projects, there are several key concepts, definitions, and resources that project managers need to know about.

Here are a few Answers to give you the basics of the book. Starting from the projects, project managers, project management, and programs

What is the formal definition of project?

A project is a temporary and unique work effort with a beginning date and an end date that creates a product, service, or result. Here's a little more detail on the key pieces of this definition:

1) Temporary, with a beginning date and an end date. A project is planned to start on a certain date and complete on a deadline, unlike maintenance or operations work, which is ongoing or perpetual.

2) Unique work effort. A team is assembled and commits to work on a specific goal, often under a contract.

3) Creates a product, service, or result. The purpose of the project is to create something that didn't exist before, often called the deliverable, which is turned over at completion to the customer (internal or external to the organization) who initiated the project.

Definition of project management and project manager

Project management, performed by a project manager, is planning, organizing, and supervising a project (i.e., a work effort that fulfills the definition of a project). Every project is unique, and there is room for creativity in how each project managers manages. But there also are many established methods, tools, and techniques that project managers use the world over.

Project managers often are either consultants or full-time employees of the company executing the project for the client (i.e., the providing organization or service provider). Often, there is a project manager on the client side as well, and the client's project manager is a counterpart to the project manager running the project on behalf of the providing organization.

It is assumed that a project manager is, to some extent, following the formal discipline of leading a project and working from a standard set of documents, especially the project plan and schedule, and using tools common to the field, such as scheduling tools and communication software.

Let's state the difference between a project and a program

Constructing a single house is a basic example of a project. By contrast, designing an entire housing complex and building all the houses, plus all of the peripherals that might be part of the complex (e.g., a parking garage or health club) would be an example of a program, which is defined as a group of related projects.

PROJECT INITIATION DOCUMENTS

A document that starts off a project

The charter is the first document created on a project. It is typically created by the project managers at the request and direction of the sponsor, who is the "money person" financing the project.

The work of a project charter

The charter provides a clear statement of what the project is supposed to accomplish, including a high-level (i.e., non-detailed) description of its goals and intended deliverables. This lays the groundwork for effective requirements gathering and, later, for properly defining the scope of the project, from which the schedule will ultimately be created.

Usually the name of the project manager assigned to the project appears in the charter along with the sponsor's name and sometimes his or her signature. The sponsor's signature is valuable, because it authorizes the project and officially permits people in the performing organization to work on the project. It also empowers the project manager, helping him or her obtain the resources needed to succeed in leading the project's activities.

Many organizations even have the policy, "If there's no charter, there's no project." This is because when projects are launched without a charter, serious problems can (and often do) arise.

Here are some examples that may sound familiar to the experienced project manager:

• Did you ever work on a project where the project manager had trouble getting resources or claiming his or her authority? Having your name on the charter as the project manager empowers you and helps you get the resources and respect you need, which is especially helpful in situations in which the power of the project manager is limited.

• Were you ever on a project that you thought were a go but were never green-lighted? Making a project official by documenting it in an authorized charter and getting the required signoffs is a way of putting the pedal to the metal and getting things going the right way.

• Did you ever work on a project where the goals or priorities were not all clearly communicated? Getting the key elements down in writing in the charter clarifies them for all of the many people who will need to know about them.

PROCESSES, PROCESS GROUPS, AND PHASES

The project management processes

An easy way to think of project management processes is as steps for managing a project. By the PMI standard, anything a PM or project team member may be working on at any given time falls into one of 47 processes. Each process typically has one main function and often one key output. For instance, the Develop Project Schedule process is all about creating the project schedule, which will outline the order and timelines of all the activities to be done over the course of the project.

The project management process groups

The 47 processes (described above) all fall into five categories PMI calls process groups:

1) Initiating processes. These are the early steps that start off a

project, including the initial request from the client and the sponsor's and (later) the project manager's early efforts to respond. They include Develop Project Charter and Identify Stakeholders.

2) Planning processes. The project manager executes these processes to plan the project.

Planning is initially based on the request to begin the project and, later, on the requirements collected from the client. Twenty-four of the processes fall into this group; including Develop Project Schedule, Plan Quality Management, Plan Procurement Management, Plan Risk Management, Plan Stakeholder Management, and many more.

3) Executing processes. This, in a nutshell, is the "giter done!" group of processes. The project manager oversees production of the deliverables the project is contracted to create and manages the employees performing this work.

Processes in this group include Direct and Manage Project Work, Conduct Procurements, Manage Stakeholder Engagement, and more.

4) Monitoring and controlling processes. This is where the project manager provides oversight. Referred to in some companies as checks and correct, this is the group of processes in which the project manager observes and measures progress against the plan and corrects where needed to keep the project under control. Processes include Control Scope, Control Schedule, Control Budget, and more.

5. Closing processes. These are the final steps a project manager completes to wrap up a project.

There are only two closing processes in the PMI model: Close Procurements and Close Project or Phase.

A phase

Phases are like subprojects within a project. Sometimes large projects are broken up into several phases. For example, on a training project broken up into two phases, Phase 1 might be the creation of a new course from designing the class to trainers' giving the first iteration of the class as a pilot. Phase 2 could be the rollout of the class as 25 sessions in one year for all employees of the company.

When projects are broken down into phases, some or all of the 47 processes are performed for each phase. Each phase can span all five of the PMI process groups, starting with (1) initiating and ending with (5) closing.

THE WORK OF PROJECT MANAGEMENT

What is a project management office, and how can it help project managers?

A project management office (PMO) is typically a team made up of some of the highly experienced project managers and senior managers at a company, who often split their project management office duties with their primary management responsibilities. Not every company is large enough for a project management office or decides to have a formal office for project management. But many companies create project management offices to help keep track of key projects and to help their project managers successfully face the many challenges that come with the job.

Here are two of the most common functions of a Project Management Office:

1) Project manager assistance

The project management office provides assistance to project managers, acting as a go-to resource where you as a project manager can find project management templates, documentation, training, and other needed support.

2) Project manager oversight

The company's projects all fall under the project management office's jurisdiction and the project managers are accountable to the project manager office.

THE THREE LEVELS OF PROJECT MANAGER

A project manager is usually in charge of managing a single project or several projects concurrently. A project manager's title might have one of three "flavors," based on increasing decision-making authority (arrows)

The project manager is the head, at the middle becomes the project coordinator, and lastly followed by project expeditor. This is a "three bears" example: one small, one big, one in the middle.

• A project expeditor has the least power.

• A project coordinator is in the middle.

• A full project manager has the most decision-making authority of the three.

Lets now look the at the role of a program manager

Role of a program manager

A program manager manages groups of related projects called programs. This also means that program managers usually supervise one or more project managers who manage the individual projects of the program.

Also, we are going to find out, what is a project portfolio, and what is the role of a project portfolio manager?

PROJECT PORTFOLIO

A project portfolio is broader than a program; it usually refers to all of the projects in a company (or to all of the projects in a large division of a company). Thus,

• Several projects make up a program.

• Multiple programs comprise a company's portfolio.

• In companies where a senior project manager is in charge of the project portfolio, he or she is called a portfolio manager.

CHAPTER 2

HOW TO BE GREAT AT A PROJECT MANAGER'S INTERVIEW

It all starts by you having that interest in project management position. Being a project manager is not a complex and hard task to be. But, it all depends with the knowhow of the subject (project management certificate) and other personal qualities that you will get to know them as you continue going through this book of enlightenment.

Before you even decide to apply for this particular kind of job, as an experienced and professional project manager, you should always have the requirements needed for you to undertake any given project. And for this reason, this book is written specifically for you who is yearning to be a progressive project manager. This is the time to be equipped with the best techniques and tips to help you get the project management job.

After you here of a project management job vacancy and it interest you, the next step is to apply for the job. You always need to complete resumes or an application forms. Later, you will need to go on an interview to meet the employers and present to them what you got.

Some people handle interviews well for others it can be a pretty traumatic experience. Even if you are the perfect match for a job vacancy if you don't prepare for your interview and put yourself across well you may never have the opportunity to prove it.

Some people seem to breeze through interviews and land jobs that they aren't even well qualified for while others find it all a horrendous struggle.

If interview technique is not your strong point don't worry; there are lots of valuable tips, tricks and advice following which will help you on your way to getting the project manager position.

HERE ARE DIFFERENT WAYS ON HOW YOU CAN BE INTERVIEWED

After you are certain that you want to be a project manager and all the necessities for the job are at your finger tips, you will feel calmed, make the right impression and ultimately succeed.

Here are a few examples of the different types of interview that you can expect and the circumstances in which you may come across them.

The Competency Based Interview

These are one of the most common interviews you will come across, focusing on the attributes and skills needed in order to fulfill the vacancy satisfactorily and basically ascertaining whether you actually possess those skills. This is where preparation and planning are essential. You need to be aware of the types of skills and attributes the interviewer will be looking for and persuade them that you are the right person for the job.

The Technical Interview

This type of interview is prevalent for people who apply for technical positions like engineering jobs or IT technicians. There's a very good chance that the interviewee will be expected to display some aspects of their technical knowledge during the interview with questions and / or tasks related to certain skills.

The Face to Face Interview

The majority (but not all) interviews are conducted face to face with video conferencing equipment coming in to play with increasing frequency these days. This will certainly happen if you have applied for that project management job overseas and it is not possible to meet up in person this can certainly be the next best thing.

The Telephone Interview

This can be used as a first stage screening process by some companies, particularly if the work will largely involve speaking on the telephone. You might have warning or the prospective employer could ring you out of the blue so be prepared for both. First impressions are extremely important so if you know that you will be contacted in this way you need to treat the telephone interview in exactly the same way as you would a face to face interview.

The Panel Interview

These are probably the most terrifying types of interview of them all. Instead of being interviewed by a single person you will have to face a whole panel of them. There is usually one person chairing the interview and other members of the panel may take turns to ask appropriate questions. It is important to direct your answer towards the member of the panel who asked the question as much as possible.

There are many different types of questions which will be put to you during an interview situation.

SOME OF THE COMMON INTERVIEW QUESTIONS ABOUT YOUR SKILLS

Here are some of the most common interview questions you are likely to come across about your personal and professional skills and how to deal with them.

Interviewers will typically ask questions about your skills like:

1) What do you regard to be your strengths?

2) What would you say are your weaknesses?

3) What can you offer our company which other candidates cannot?

4) What would your friends and colleagues say are your best qualities?

5) Why should we give you the job?

All interviewers really need to know, if you are the best person for the job.

It is important that you know your strengths and talk about whatever strengths you have which are relevant to the position you have applied for. The interviewer won't be interested in just a long list o f skills; he'll also want you to take things one step further.

Always in an interview, the interviewer is always eager to know if you posses other personal qualities apart from the skilled needed for the project.

Below are some of nine qualities and key characteristics the interviewer will typically be looking for including:

1) Communication and the ability to get along with a variety of different people in the organization.

2) A good work ethic – an interviewer will be searching for someone who is honest, hard working, polite, reliable and co-operates well with others

3) Team work – is often important to have the ability to be an effective member of the team as well as able to step up to the mark as a competent team leader if needed

4) Full knowledge of modern technology – this is a pre-requisite of the majority of positions in the modern work place

5) Problem solving skills – being able to identify solutions using your own initiative

6) Enthusiasm – positive energy breeds success. Employers love enthusiastic employees

7) Determination – they need to know that you are focused and determined to achieve goals

8) Quick learner – even if you don't have experience in some matters for the position, being a quick learner means that you will be able to take on a variety of new tasks

9) Flexibility – the best workers are those who show the flexibility to fulfill a variety of roles and tasks in pursuit of a common goal

Don't go overboard about your weaknesses. Everybody has one so choose a minor chink in your armor which isn't essential for the job you are being interviewed for. Turn this weakness from negative to a positive and show how you have worked on the weakness to turn it around.

THE IMPORTANCE OF BODY LANGUAGE AT INTERVIEWS

It's not only the things you say in an interview which are important; it's also the way that you simultaneously in cooperate both the saying and body language. Body language is incredibly important and can have a powerful impact on the way that someone perceives you. This means that you have to be on your guard from the second you step onto the premises. Your body language will be giving tell-tale signs about you long before you open your mouth to speak.

Here are a few handy tips to make sure that your body language is saying the right things.

Make Eye Contact

This shows the interviewer that you are really listening and paying attention to what they are saying. There's a difference between making eye contact and staring with a blank expression at the interviewers eyes but do try to hold eye contact for just a few seconds each time you make it.

If there is a panel of interviewers, do make sure that you hold eye contact with each one of them individually, starting and finishing with the member of the panel who asked each particular question.

Slouching

Slouching and a bad posture send out all of the wrong messages. Hunching forward is not good but neither is lounging around with arms and legs spread out in all directions. Try to not to clench your fist tightly in your lap but on the other hand it's not a good idea to look too relaxed either. Be aware of your posture from the minute you step through the door into reception. Don't sit pointing towards the door as you wait for your appointment, it will look like you're planning your escape route. Remember to sit up straight leaning slightly forwards when you are asked a question to make you appear attentive and curious.

Using Your Hands

Hands are one of the biggest giveaways when it comes to body language so pay particular attention to what you do with them. If you touch your fingertips together it suggests authority but don't overdo it. Sit with your hands in your lap and try not to wave them around when making a point. It just gives the impression that a person is unpredictable and nervous. Try not to clench your fists and certainly don't bite your nails because it is incredibly distracting and will make you look like a nervous wreck. This is not the image you need to portray at all.

Avoid Touching Your Face

Try not to touch your face during the interview. People who sit rubbing their noses or fiddling with their hair gives the appearance of being untrustworthy and dishonest. You should also resist the temptation to rub your neck or head which can make you look bored. Crossing your arms is not the perfect solution to stop you from doing these things however, that just makes you look unapproachable and defensive.

Sit up, relax your shoulders and turn slightly towards the interviewer to make sure that they are really listening to you and taking notice of what you say.

Remember to Smile

This is important even if you are having an interview over the telephone. Did you know that you can hear a smile? Well, it's true. Be ready to smile at the appropriate times and don't be afraid to laugh if the interviewer does. This shows that you have a little personality and are not just a scared robot.

Don't Fidget

Fidgeting and moving around are signs of impatience and boredom so remember, no jiggling your feet around or tapping your fingers on the chair of the arm. Plant both feet on the floor firmly, sit up straight and focus your attentions on the interviewer.

Mirroring Is Good

Matching the positive body language of your interviewer can help you to get in their good books. Try to be subtle about it; any bold movements will possibly frighten the poor interviewer half to death. If you mirror the odd nod or posture shift it can help to break the ice.

Handshakes

Handshakes should be handled with care. Too strong or firm will make you appear arrogant and took weak and limp will make you seem like a pushover.

It is also important to respect the personal space of your interviewer. Although, the first impressions are the ones which count the most it's also important to make a graceful exit. Look interested, adopt a confident posture and hold your head high from the minute you step through the door into reception until the second you are far enough away to relax.

PREPARING FOR A PROJECT MANAGER JOB INTERVIEW

An interview provides you with an opportunity to showcase your qualification to an employer, so it pays to be well prepared. Here are tips and hints to fully help you with an interview success.

WHEN PREPARING

•Try to know the name of the organization

•Review your requirements and credentials for the vacancy.

•You will always be asked to express yourself and bring to light all your experience.

YOUR PERSONAL APPEARANCE TELLS MORE ABOUT YOU

•Be well groomed

•Dress appropriately

•Avoid chewing gum

START PLANNING AS EARLY AS POSSIBLE

You need to start thinking about answers to the most common questions asked in interviews. The interviewer will probably start off the proceedings asking questions like "tell me all about yourself" or "tell me about your resume" these are designed to ease you into the interview as well as help the interviewer learn a little bit about you. Make sure that you're ready with some good answers.

It's important to get the balance right when you start to talk about yourself.

The response needs to be quite short with a good strong opening line about your current position, the years you have held the position and a brief rundown of the professional journey which took you there.

If your resume has a few gaps or is full of short term jobs don't worry too much about it but do have a few answers and explanations ready because that is something which is bound to be noticed.

Have a careful read through the person / job specification and identify the particular skills which you have which demonstrate that you are a perfect fit for this position. Try writing down your answers and reading them aloud to yourself. It's often a good idea to interview yourself in front of a mirror and record your answers just to see how you come across from both sides of the table.

Soon after the introductions there will undoubtedly be a few tricky questions thrown in and you should expect something like "where do you see your career taking you in four or five year's time" or "what would you describe as your weaknesses". Make sure that you have good answers readily prepare –there'll be more of that later.

Before you attend the interview you need to do lots of background research and fact finding about the company. Scour their website, read the news stories and learn as much as you can about the profile of the company. You need to have a plausible reason why you will be an asset to their company and if you don't have much knowledge of the company you can hardly sound plausible.

THE NIGHT BEFORE YOU FOR THAT JOB INTERVIEW

Make sure that you take the time to relax the night before the interview so that you get plenty of valuable rest and don't try to cram with last minute information. This will only lead to panic which is not the best state to be in when you arrive at the interview.

Prepare your outfit the night before and make sure that all your clothes and items needed for that interview are in a good shape. Looking good can really help to boost your confidence which is essential if you want to make a good impression.

Work out your travel plans and timings. It's always best to plan your arrival a good ten minutes before your designated interview time. It can be beneficial to take a half hour to sit, read through the schedule one more time and arrive calm and confident at your interview destination.

THE DAY FOR THE INTERVIEW

•Be early

•Try to find out the name of the person who is interviewing you and give him or her gentle hand shake.

•settle down and respond to each query concisely

•Use proper English and always avoid slag

•Be cooperative and enthusiastic

•Always thank the interviewer when you leave and shake hands.

CHAPTER 3

PROJECT PLANNING

As a project manager, planning, setting up measures and schedules are key mandatory's factors to consider for a successful project. A project is supposed to be a unique endeavor that represents a change to an organization; a plan becomes the road map of how to get there. Without a good project plan, the project becomes lost.

Creating a project management plan is perhaps the most important thing that a project manager can do as the project management plan describes how all aspects of the project will be approached.

By considering each area, you are forced to think about each area and you will inevitably discover important information that would otherwise have been missed. The team should be included in the creation of the plan and the plan should be considered a living document that will be adjusted as the project progresses. The project management plan is a useful tool for the project manager as well as the rest of the project team, the customer, and management.

While setting up project plans, here are some measures to consider.

Use High-Touch, Low-Tech Methods as Much as Possible

There is a tendency today to rely on software and digital communication to accomplish much of the work required in project management. While these tools can be very effective, they tend to reduce the opportunities for team involvement. In addition to being detrimental to the development of an optimal working team, this also tends to result in a lower quality product as the team has less input and loses the benefit of their collective knowledge.

The next time you're developing a schedule, task list, Work Breakdown Structure (WBS), or other project related documentation try this. Gather the team in a conference room and use whiteboards, post-it notes, poster paper and markers, and involve the entire team in the collaborative process. You will be amazed at the level of discussion and debate that develops as the team members cover the walls with post-it notes and debate the sequence or duration of tasks as they remove and reposition notes around the room. This debate and discussion will often reveal hidden problems or issues that would otherwise have been missed. In addition, it will also increase the probability that all work is identified and accounted for, avoiding problems down the road.

This approach also encourages buy-in and commitment from the team, builds a positive team environment, and brings some fun back into the workplace.

Use Retrospectives as Tools for Continuous Improvement

The retrospective is a practice that comes from the agile methodologies but one that can be very useful in the traditional project management world as well. The retrospective is a process-centric meeting that includes only project team members and is focused on how work was done, what went well, what could be improved, what could be added, and what should be dropped. Often the retrospective is facilitated by writing three questions (what went well, what went less well, what can we add or drop) on a whiteboard and letting discussion begin.

In the agile world, work is typically done in iterations of two- or three-week durations. The retrospective meeting is held at the end of each iteration with the intent of examining how the work process went during the iteration and how to make improvements for the next iteration. While we don't typically schedule work in iterations in the traditional world, we can still conduct retrospectives periodically, as a tool for continuous improvement.

The key to the retrospective is to encourage candid input from all team members, as everyone on the team is required to participate. Another important requirement for conducting a productive retrospective is that it will not be attended by anyone outside the team – especially not by anyone in a management position. The reason for this is to ensure that you get candid input from all team members. Some team members can be intimidated by the presence of outsiders, particularly those from management, and may be reluctant to speak up especially regarding something that is not working well, so you should restrict attendance in order to encourage full and candid participation.

Create a Work Breakdown Structure (WBS) – Always

A WBS is an essential project management tool that is extremely helpful in managing and controlling the work of the project as that work unfolds.

The main purpose of the WBS is to capture all the work required by the project. Once this is accomplished we have a tool to use to help ensure that the team is only working on tasks required by (and accounted for in schedule and budget) the project. In addition, the graphic form of the WBS can be easily color coded and posted in the team work area to show tasks completed, in progress, and remaining. This color coded WBS is a great way to continuously communicate project status to management and other stakeholders.

The WBS is automatically generated by most common project management software packages (i.e. MS Project) or with the addition of inexpensive add-on software (Chart Pro). Software makes the creation of a completely customizable WBS easy and mostly automatic, so there is no reason for any PM to go without this extremely useful project management tool.

Take the Time to Create a Detailed Scope Statement

If you ask someone who heads up an organization what his or her biggest headache is regarding project work, the likely answer will be "everything costs more than they say it will cost and everything takes longer than they say it will take." This common response is mostly caused by scope creep, the unintentional (and therefore uncontrolled) growth of project scope. While scope creep has a number of causes, the most common is a failure to adequately define scope at the beginning of the project.

If the scope is not adequately defined, it becomes extremely difficult to create an accurate budget and schedule and the project is likely doomed from the start. In addition, without an adequately defined scope the change control process becomes problematic as it is challenging to determine if a requested change is within scope or out of scope if the project scope isn't well defined.

Under these conditions it becomes almost impossible to manage a project to a planned budget and schedule.

Always take the time to adequately define the project scope during the planning process and always involve the entire team in that effort. Defining scope will be an iterative effort involving the entire project team; however, the time spent will be well worth it as it will greatly increase the probability of project success.

Take the Time to Do a Thorough Requirements Analysis

Few things are more frustrating than being in a position where you are arguing with the customer over whether or not a specific feature or capability is required on the project (even more so if the feature or capability in question is missing). Taking the time to do a thorough requirement analysis is something that is (unfortunately) not done in many projects.

Most projects will have some form of written requirements (although a surprising number do not) but a thorough analysis is often not done. It is very important that the project team has a clear understanding of all project requirements and it is equally important that the customer has that same understanding and that both sides are in agreement.

Many times, especially on large or complex projects, there are requirements that can be costly to meet in terms of time and resources. Sometimes these requirements are not necessary at all, but this determination cannot be made without conducting a thorough requirements analysis that involves both the project team and the customer. Additionally, project requirements that are initially missed and then need to be added later tend to be costly in terms of both time and money, in addition to the cost of the strained relationship between the team and the customer.

Take the time to do thorough requirements analysis involving both the project and customer teams and enjoy a happier, and more successful, project experience.

Embrace Procrastination – Delay Decisions to the Last Responsible Moment

This is a concept borrowed from the agile methodologies that can be very useful in traditional project management as well. The key phrase here is "responsible moment" which doesn't mean that we wait until the last possible moment but that we wait until the moment where delaying any longer would cause us to lose a viable option.

Oftentimes we make a decision and take a particular action that turns out to be incorrect and requires additional work to undo the results or correct a problem, caused by that incorrect decision. This happens, in many cases, because we make the decision based on incomplete information due to pressure to take action and move forward. Typically, we learn more about our work as we move through the project and by delaying decisions to the last responsible moment, we reduce the likelihood of making a bad decision based on incomplete information as we will now have more information and a better understanding of the situation.

Delay decisions until the last responsible moment and reduce amount of wasted effort on your project.

Set and Maintain a Sustainable Pace for Your Project Team

If your team is routinely working long hours during the week (ten plus hours per day) and coming in on the weekend to "catch up when it is quiet," then you have a problem that needs to be resolved. There will always be the occasional (note: occasional) crisis or problem that will require team members to stay late or come in on the weekend. But this should be the exception rather than the rule and these occurrences should be few and far between. You should also acknowledge that when this happens, 90% of the time, it will be because the project manager made a mistake.

A professional and enlightened project manager should be working hard to create a work environment that encourages the team to be engaged, motivated, innovative, and all the other qualities we expect in a high performing team. Nothing will destroy this positive work environment more quickly than working continuous long hours and weekends over extended periods. When this begins to happen, the project manager needs to examine resource loading and schedule (and scope to be sure the team is working only on WBS items and that the WBS is complete), and make whatever adjustments necessary to relieve the situation.

People need balance between work and life (this is not just a corporate slogan, but is actually reality) to stay sharp and motivated and to recharge so that they can continue to be productive members of a high performing team.

The ultimate price paid for not correcting an overwork situation is that the best people will begin to leave as they know their worth and they know that they have other opportunities and do not have to work in a "sweatshop" environment. Maintain a sustainable work pace and enjoy the benefits of working on a high performing team.

Ensure That Your Requirements are Well Written

Since you've taken the time to do a thorough requirement analysis, you should also take the additional time to ensure that each requirement is written properly. By written properly we mean that the requirement is specific such that if several people read the requirement it is not possible for any one of them to derive a meaning different from that of anyone else. Everyone who reads a requirement should come away with the same meaning; if they don't, the requirement needs to be rewritten.

The requirement also needs to be definitively measurable or

verifiable. For example, a requirement that states that something should be "as light as possible" is poorly written because "light as possible" is open to interpretation and is not definitively verifiable. Take the time to ensure that your requirements are well written. Avoid rework and wasted effort as well as situations that will strain the relationship between you and the customer.

Always Include a WBS Dictionary with Your WBS

A WBS dictionary is a document that includes pertinent information for each item in the WBS, including a detailed description of what the task involves, exit criteria (how do we know it's done), percent complete criteria (how do we measure percent complete), constraints, assumptions, and any other information that we believe to be germane to that item. PMI describes the WBS as a separate document but this information can easily be included in the task notes of each item on your MS Project schedule. However you decide to do it, be sure to capture and document important, defining information for each item in the WBS, and avoid potentially costly and embarrassing problems later in the project.

Create and Use a Stakeholder Register

Failing to identify an important project stakeholder is something that is completely avoidable, yet is often the cause of grief and unhappiness for many project managers. When a stakeholder is overlooked, it usually results in that stakeholder not receiving pertinent information that he or she is expecting.

When that information is not received, it is unlikely that the stakeholder will choose the easiest solution and contact the Project Manager to request it. It is much more likely that the stakeholder will do nothing and fume over the lack of information, telling herself stories to explain the lack of communication. At some point this unhappiness will boil over, resulting in an angry call to the PM or to the PM's boss regarding the situation.

As a project manager you should take the time to identify all project stake holders, anyone who can impact or be impacted by your project and record this information in a stakeholder register. In addition, you should determine each stakeholder's level of interest, what information they expect, how often they expect information, what level of detail and format they need, and incorporate that knowledge into your communications management plan. Happy stakeholders will make your project management experience much more enjoyable.

A plan is always made by other plans to help it work well and smoothly

COMMUNICATIONS MANAGEMENT PLAN

The communications management plan is a critical project management tool that is frequently overlooked. Good communications begin with a good plan. Identify everyone who needs to receive project information and determine what level of detail they expect and how often they expect to receive the information. In addition, determine the best method of delivery for each individual (email, formal report, face to face, etc.) and create a written communications management plan, as a section of your project management plan, that will describe how, when, and what will be communicated to each individual.

Many project managers fail to take the time to write up a formal plan, thinking they have all this information in their head and know exactly what to do. The reality is that they don't know nearly as much as they think they do and once the project work gets underway, they'll find themselves extremely busy and communications will be one of the first areas to suffer. This causes unnecessary problems for the project manager and the project. Do yourself a favor and always take the time to create a communications management plan.

RISK MANAGEMENT PLAN

All projects have risk, and risk will always exist, whether you choose to manage it or not. While there will always be events that occur during a project that could not have been foreseen, the truth is that most bad things that happen on projects could have been avoided had the team taken the time to talk about the "possibilities" at the beginning of the project. This discussion is exactly what risk planning is, and unfortunately, this is also a step that is skipped by many project managers.

By taking the time to do risk planning, you will greatly reduce the number of fire drills that you will have to run during the project. Risk planning will significantly increase the probability that your project will complete on time and on budget. In addition, responses to risk events, that your team comes up with in a relaxed early planning stage, are likely to be significantly better than solutions they come up with when forced to deal with a crisis during the heat of the project. Take the time to incorporate proper risk management and enjoy a significantly higher probability of success.

SCHEDULE MANAGEMENT PLAN

Apply the 40 Hour Rule when Creating Your Project Schedule

When developing the project schedule, the project manager should never include any task that requires more than 40 hours to complete. Human nature being what it is, if you assign someone a task that is scheduled to take five weeks, you will likely hear that everything is going well and on schedule for week's one through four. At some point around week four, you will probably hear that we are not going to make our week five completion date, leaving you no time to do anything to avoid the missed deadline. The reason for this is that most people procrastinate or are heavily loaded with work and will tend to get behind early on.

With a five week completion schedule most people will also feel that they will be able to catch up, which most of the time, probably won't turn out to be the case. Better to break that five week task into five one week tasks so that if things start to fall behind at week two, you will know and have time to get help for the struggling team member or offload some tasks to keep the project on schedule.

CHAPTER 4

CONFLICT RESOLUTION MEASURES

This chapter deals with conflict resolution, which, like risk management, is a method of problem solving within the scope of the overall project. Conflict may be considered by some theorists to be inherent in the course of human interaction. In essence, conflict is a type of risk, because, left unresolved, it could jeopardize the future of your project. Unfortunately, it is not a risk you can usually mitigate in advance since you do not usually know where such conflict will arise. However, if you're putting together a team, you can make an effort to include people who you know generally get along with one another.

Cooperative Resolution

The idea of cooperative conflict behavior suggests that parties work together to resolve their conflict. This, however, assumes that both parties are willing to enter into a cooperative agreement. Getting two sides to sit down and cooperate is easier said than done. In any group situation there is also the potential for competitive conflicts, which perpetuate and lead to greater problems.

As a project manager, you will have to address the need for cooperation while understanding that there may be a degree of competition involved at the root of a conflict. Often, conflict is also the result of attitudes, or a belief system embodied within the individual long before the project was ever initiated. Such prejudgments are often at the root of an impending conflict. There may also be self-doubt and lack of confidence in one's own abilities. Interacting with others who may be more confident or highly skilled can intensify these insecurities.

Conflict is often the result of uncertainty or miscommunication. Frequently, someone has simply neglected to include all of the details in their communications to another team member, or procedures or even intent was misunderstood.

To nip potential conflicts in the bud, a project manager needs to look for signs that team members:

•Are lacking in self-confidence or displaying uncertainty about tasks or procedures

•Are unsure of what their functions are, which often the result of miscommunication.

•Are predisposed to disregard authority, or have a prejudicial attitude toward others.

•Are consumed by a competitive nature (although sometimes a healthy competition can be positive for a project)

Are motivated by their personal agendas at the expense of the project

IDENTIFYING KEY CHARACTERS

Certain characteristics distinguish different types of individuals. You will likely discover some of these common types on your team:

•Tigers intimidate others by holding a degree of power over them. Often insecure about their own role, tigers will use any leverage they can, from a bully threatening to beat up a classmate to a manager who threatens to fire anyone who dares question his or her authority.

Watch who you put in positions of authority, and make sure they has the necessary people skills.

•Prima donnas display inflated egos and a misguided sense of self-importance. These types can be condescending toward others and are often working with a personal agenda. Your best resource is to let them enjoy a false sense of importance as long as it does not impinge on the project.

•Passive-aggressive types operate in a quiet manner, yet communicate calculated or manipulated messages through judgmental comments, body language, well-placed guilt, playing the martyr, or displaying an attitude that often seems aloof or unconcerned. The more aggressive and obvious version of the passive-aggressive is the brown-noser, who is always trying to appease the right person to score points and satisfy his or her own need for importance. Passively try to maintain control with the passive-aggressive and stay a few steps ahead of the brown-noser.

•People-pleasers will do whatever is necessary for praise and a much-needed ego boost. They simply have a more basic need for approval than the brown-noser, who has an agenda. Let the people-pleaser know you are pleased with his or her efforts.

And finally, you'll encounter the legitimate team player, who is; at least as far as you're concerned, comfortable with himself or herself and content within the parameters of the project and the people with whom he or she is working. Yes, you'll have team members who will simply come to the project to work hard and interact socially (or not). If you're lucky, this will be the majority of your team or at least they will appear as such throughout the duration of the project. After all, your primary concern is how they interact with you and the project team. A bully on the ball field or a manipulator at home is not your concern in the project environment.

Assessing the Conflict Situation

Now you know the characters, so what do you do when conflict rears its ugly head? First, you will need to assess the nature of the conflict and who the featured players are. A conflict can manifest itself at various levels:

•Is it a conflict between two individuals on the project team?

•Is it a conflict between two groups of individuals?

•Is it a conflict between one individual and the rest of the team?

•Is it a conflict between one individual and management, sponsors, stakeholders, or you?

•Is it a conflict of a moral or ethical nature, between one or more team members and their beliefs?

•Is there a conflict between your team and an outside source?

Conflict is not always two team members not getting along. Several variations on the theme of conflict can arise within a project. There are also levels of disagreement, ranging from petty arguments to threats, legal action, or violence.

Gathering the necessary facts is essential to successfully resolving a conflict.

One side of the story, and sometimes both sides, will not provide the entire picture if the conflict is based on an occurrence or series of activities. Make sure you find out all the details before taking action.

You, therefore, need to assess who the conflict is between and its level of severity. You also need to assess where this conflict fits in the scheme of the project. Does it stem from something internal? Is the argument over the process that the project is following, or is the dispute about politics, parking spaces, or another issue that is external to the actual project but causing friction or tension that is affecting the success of the project?

Conflicts frequently arise during the initiation phase of the project based on scheduling, task assignments, work distribution, and clarity of the tasks to be performed. Often, people disagree about how long a task should take, or because they are being given more of the workload than someone else. As the project progresses, the team generally settles into a comfortable rhythm and adapts to each of the varying personalities, but at the beginning, team members can be resentful if they feel they are carrying more of the weight. This occurs most frequently in volunteer projects when there is nothing personal at stake. In these cases, the best you can do is remind the individual of the value of his own work and diminish the concern about what others are or aren't doing.

Before returning to how to deal with the various configurations of conflicts mentioned earlier, let's look at several ways to successfully manage them.

METHODS OF CONFLICT RESOLUTION

Mediation

Mediation is a method of resolving conflict in which a neutral third party intervenes to try to settle a dispute between two parties. You as an open minded project manager, you ought to act as an intermediary if the conflict is between two members in the team.

Meditation is one of methods to solving conflicts among your team members. Using meditation as a way to solving conflicts, you as project manager act as neutral party between the two conflicting members. Hopefully, you can find a middle ground that allows each side to walk away satisfied with the outcome. If the situation is a clear-cut, win-lose argument, such as whether to use program A or B, you need to make a clear decision and explain that it is based solely on the factors involved and not the individuals.

Conflict Transformation

A more complicated process called conflict transformation uses mediation, but focuses on the attitudes and perceptions of the parties and looks to alter these perceptions. On small-scale or short-term projects, the time frame won't allow this level of resolution to make radical changes in personalities. Long-term, large-scale projects with significant impact on a wide-spread population may require loftier resolution techniques in which the parties are encouraged to look beyond the project to their feelings and attitudes. Conflict transformation is concerned primarily with changing the attitudes and perceptions the parties have about one another. In the long term, this can be very beneficial, as changed attitudes can result in less conflict moving forward. For instance, television programs designed to teach youngsters how to properly accept and understand other people use the same techniques. Moralistic in nature, they work with adults too, but success is often harder to achieve since attitudes are more firmly embedded within adults.

To achieve such transformation, you may need the help of outside professionals to get to the root of the conflict. Compromise is a key factor in conflict resolution. Once again, as in any mediation, both parties need to be amenable.

Parties will need to sit down and negotiate a settlement that is satisfactory to both sides. In a situation that doesn't present a clear-cut decision, a compromise is often the result of mediation.

CHAPTER 5

THE NEED FOR MOTIVATION IN A PROJECT

To motivate is to stimulate to action by providing an incentive or a motive. Real motivation, however, is more than just action; it is based on an attitude.

The drive to succeed, learn, grow, and attain a goal is motivation. Personal investment in a product, activity, or outcome will motivate individuals also. As a project manager, you need to keep your team motivated, focused on completing the project, and achieving the team goal. From wise words to cash rewards, motivation comes in many forms. You can use several techniques with your team, but the best two come from you: be creative and be sincere.

What Motivates Us?

For people to feel vested in a project, they need to see the big picture and look at the project from a global perspective. This big-picture view needs to be established from the onset. Projects are not usually successful if the people involved are not aware of the ultimate goal. The more a person is attached to or feels involved with the overall project, the more motivated he or she will be to work harder.

Motivation is not something you use only when the project is going downhill or has fallen behind schedule. Proper motivation should be established from the start of the project. You want to put together a championship team from the beginning. To do this you need to:

•Seek out personalities that work well with others.

•Bring everyone together in an introductory meeting.

•Present the broad picture of the project and the impact it will have on other people.

•Establish a team identity.

•Let others know what this team plans to accomplish on the project. Spread the word — present the team and their mission to the larger group, be it the company, or the whole organization.

Motivational Theories

Motivation takes on various forms. Internal motivation could be satisfaction from a job well done, an inner sense of fulfillment, or the sense of doing for others. External motivation includes material goods, awards, recognition, and of course, money. The nature of the project, the sponsor, and the setting of the project will dictate which, if any, external motivating factors you can offer. On every project, you can try to inspire team members to seek internal rewards along with the external rewards.

To motivate others to perform, you need a basic understanding of human nature. Many people in leadership positions do not fully understand the basic elements of motivational thinking as it pertains to others. Motivation can be an individual factor. Although a desire for monetary rewards is somewhat common, one person may be motivated by a possible new title or promotion while another may simply want more time to spend at home with the family.

Unfortunately, an enthusiastic leader often assumes that the motivating factors that propelled him to his level of success are the same for everyone else. It's as if they think, "I became a manager, so why everyone else should not try to work their way up to the same lofty position?" This is not a broad-based view of what motivates others.

CHAPTER 6

ADDITIONAL USEFUL TECHNIQUES FOR A PROJECT MANAGER

Keep All Your Project Documents Current

One of the reasons that many of these critical documents are not created by a number of project managers is the opinion that creating the documents is just "busy work" and that the documents add no value. This opinion can actually be true if documents are not kept current and are allowed to become so out of date as to be useless.

Remember that these documents are meant to be tools that are regularly updated and utilized throughout the life of the project. A schedule that is not updated and is so incorrect after six months that it can no longer be used to help guide the project adds no value and the work that went into creating it was just wasted. The same can be said for a risk register, project management plan, communications management plan and any number of critical project management documents.

Always keep project management documents updated and current. Use them as they were intended, to help guide the work of the project to a successful conclusion.

Don't Think in the Short Term; Take the Long View When Making Decisions

One of the most self destructive practices in which organizations engage is the practice of short-term thinking. For instance, the focus on short-term revenues is probably the cause of more problems and outright failures in organizations than any other single practice. The effects of short-term thinking can also be detrimental to the success of a project, if the project manager chooses that path.

Avoid danger and always take the long view in all decisions related to your project. Consider the long-term development of your team when planning, training and encourage coaching and mentoring opportunities. Encourage sharing of knowledge and cross-training among team members and discourage hoarding of knowledge and unhealthy competition between team members. Actively recruit team members (and employees when you have the opportunity), who fit in and support a healthy workplace culture by encouraging your team to help others in the organization, whenever possible. Taking this approach will make both your team and organization stronger and more successful.

Create and Use a "Lessons Learned Log" from the First Day of Your Project

The lessons learned log is another valuable project management tool that is frequently overlooked. The lessons learned log is a great way to record knowledge gained through doing project work and when used correctly, can save time, money, and avoid many of the problems experienced during the project.

This may come as a surprise, but the mistakes and other unpleasant things that your team experienced on the project were probably not original work. In other words, they were probably experienced by other teams on other projects. By taking the time to record these events along with their root causes and recovery actions, you can help project teams avoid repeating these mistakes in the future.

An organization with mature project management processes will require not only the creation and use of a lessons learned log throughout the project, but a review of that information during the initiation processes of a new project. One last point regarding lessons learned: Resist the temptation to create the lessons learned documen t as part of the closing processes of the project. To gain the most from the effort, the lessons learned log should be populated during the project as the "lessons are learned." The memory is much more vivid and the facts will be more accurate if they are recorded as the event occurs. Post the log on the project website or in the project folder and encourage your team to add to it regularly.

Think in Terms of Win/Win Rather Than in Terms of Tradeoffs

As a project manager you will have the opportunity to m ake decisions on a daily basis. Some of these decisions will be relatively minor while others will be much more important with potentially significant consequences.

As a decision maker, you should try to develop a win/win approach rather than a tradeoff approach to decisions. In other words, try to develop both/ and construct rather than an if/then or either/or construct to your decision making. There is almost always a path where both parties can benefit from a specific decision, and if you can develop the habit of looking for that path in all your decisions, you and your team will be much more successful.

Be conscious that a win/win approach isn't a compromise (where both parties lose something and real commitment is unlikely), but the search for a truly better decision, where both sides benefit. The win/win approach definitely takes more effort and probably more time, (at least at first until it becomes more natural for you) but the payoff is well worth the extra effort.

Create a Risk Register and Use it throughout the Life of the Project

A risk register is simply a list of all the possible things that can go wrong on a project, plus the relevant information needed to monitor and manage these potential events.

Many people skip the step of creating a formal risk register, believing they know and understand the risks, and believe that the effort needed to document and manage risk is excessive. This simply isn't true, and these people are individuals whose days seem to go from one crisis to another, as they work through the project.

The greatest value of creating and using the risk register is that it gets the team to brainstorm potential events on the project multiple times. The process is iterative and lasts through the life of the project as risk changes throughout the project. Additionally, this process always turns up items that would have otherwise been missed. This process also helps build the team and makes everyone more knowledgeable regarding the work of the project, resulting in a stronger team and a more successful project.

Create a Naturally Motivating Environment Rather than Trying to Motivate Individuals

As a project manager, you rarely will have control over salaries (or over many of the dysfunctional behaviors that are likely occurring within your organization), but you will have a fair amount of influence regarding the work environment of your project team. Make an effort to provide your team with as much individual autonomy over their work as possible. Also as a leader, frequently reinforce the purpose of the work and the benefits the work is producing for the organization, customers, and (hopefully) society. Finally, provide opportunities for members of your team to grow professionally (and personally) through opportunities such as training, seminars, college courses, and mentoring. Do these things and motivation will take care of itself.

Develop the Knowledge Workers on Your Team

"Knowledge workers" is a term increasingly used to describe the type of people we are increasingly seeing in today's workforce, people who have to think and be creative or innovative in order to do their jobs. But the term can have a broader meaning to include anyone who is engaged and brought into the decision-making process regarding their work. It is this broader definition that we are concerned with here.

You should strive to include or draw your team into as much of the decision making process of the project as possible. Remember no one knows more about the work of the project than the people who are actually doing the work, so do everything you can to involve them to the greatest extent possible.

By trusting your team with as much of this responsibility as possible, you will see motivation, commitment, and performance increase significantly (and for the long term), benefiting the organization as well as the project. While there is some risk to this approach, the benefits far outweigh the occasional problem that may result from a less than optimal decision.

Encourages Conflict – Just Be Sure it's the Right Kind of Conflict

Conflict is actually a good thing for a project team, as long as conflict remains focused on ideas and is not allowed to become personal. Spirited debate around ideas brings out the best of what your team has to offer their experience, knowledge, and insight into the work at hand. By encouraging conflict around ideas, you will consistently get the most innovative and creative ideas the team can produce.

While conflict concerning ideas can be very beneficial, conflict centered on people or personalities can be extremely destructive and should not be tolerated by the project manager or anyone on the team. Personal attacks or ridicule of team members (in public or in private) is completely inappropriate in the workplace and should be addressed and stopped immediately.

Utilize Both Project Management Experience and Formal Education and Training to Accomplish Professional Growth

Often times I'll hear working project managers espouse the benefits of experience while discounting the need for formal training or education. The argument is typically along the lines of "I've been doing this for 25 years and I've learned everything I need to know on the job." These are usually the same people who will tell you that everything is always late and over budget and the level of stress is always very high because that's just the nature of project management.

Unfortunately, a person having experience alone usually means that the individual spent a great deal of time learning and reinforcing bad habits, and is likely not an effective project manager. It's equally detrimental to just have theory alone, as someone with formal training but no real-world experience will lack the ability to temper the theory and apply that knowledge in a real-world workplace environment.

The best way to develop professionally is to continuously seek formal project management training while gaining experience in the workplace. By taking this approach an individual can learn the principles or mechanics of project management (i.e., why things work the way they do) and apply only the tools and techniques that add value for a particular organization, thus optimizing performance and professional growth.

Create and Maintain an Issue Log

An issue log is also known to many people as an action item list. The two can be very similar, if not identical. An issue log is intended to track issues that arise during a project and which, for any number of reasons, cannot be re- solved immediately.

The issue log typically lists the date the issue was discovered, who reported it, a brief description of the issue, status of the issue, the individual responsible for resolving the issue, and an expected resolution date. The log is reviewed regularly and issues are monitored until they are resolved and closed out.

The issue log is one of those tools that seem like common sense, yet isn't always common practice. How many times have you attended a meeting where several new action items were created and assigned, but not documented and were never heard of again? Because of the heavy workload under which most people are working and the many complexities of the workplace, issues that are not documented and tracked to conclusion are likely to disappear temporarily, only to reappear as a bigger problem at a later date. Always create and use an issue log.

Plan and Conduct Meetings Correctly and with Purpose

One of the most methods and techniques which are used to uplift a company and make it extremely successful is planning and conducting meetings. The theory is based on the idea that this will leave people in attendance those who are truly interested and have a stake in the meeting subject with a focus in their mind on how to effectively execute their tasks. How would this work with your current employer? My guess is that there would be a lot of one-person meetings. Meetings are often not effective and that really doesn't need to be the case.

Always create an agenda for your meeting, distribute the agenda to the attendees prior to the meeting (along with some incentive for them to actually read the agenda and come to the meeting prepared), and stick to the agenda during the meeting. Also, be very specific as to the reason for the meeting and who should attend. Meetings should be held to address a specific issue (never to gather status) and should only involve those required to discuss or resolve that issue. These two practices alone will produce a significant improvement in the quality of your meetings.

Never Use Meetings as a Method for Gathering Project Status

Weekly status meeting should be common occurrence, and should worth the cost in time and lost productivity. A weekly team meeting that is focused on status could easily run for ninety minutes and go much longer if it is allowed to devolve into discussions related to current technical issues on the project. These meetings will absolutely kill the morale of busy project team members who are fuming as they sit in a meeting they perceive as having little value while worrying about all the work they should be doing.

There are many effective ways for a project manager to gather project status. One of the best methods is to have team members submit a brief status by email each week. These individual submissions can then be summarized by the PM and posted for team members to read at their leisure. Another approach is to have the PM meet individually or in small groups of two or three team members and (again) summarize reported status and post results for future reading. Always try to be conscious of the workload and time pressures felt by your team. Plan meetings that are productive, brief, and few in number as possible.

Always Document Phone Conversations and Verbal Agreements

This is another practice that many times falls by the wayside due to the pressures of workload and time. However, this tip pays off frequently, when consistently applied. The reason for documenting phone conversations and verbal agreements is not so much a CYA thing as it is a way to remember and know what was said or agreed to in a conversation.

Think of the number of phone conversations and hallway discussions that you experience in a typical day. How many involve an action or agreement that was to be enacted? Now fast forward three weeks, and try to imagine recalling details of phone and hallway conversations. You can probably see the problem.

Document these calls and conversations in a log (on a device or on paper) and get in the habit of reviewing the log periodically. You'll be surprised how many little things you'll catch before they turn into big things.

Involve End Users as Early as Possible in the Requirements Gathering Process

End users oftentimes have the best perspective on the requirements necessary to make a product or service successful. Let's say for instance, you were once a project manager for a particular company and you are involved in projects where you are in close and frequent contact with the customer team, which typically consist of a number of highly trained, experienced technical people. These people are well-versed in the technical aspects of the product, the mission, and what is needed to accomplish their goals. What is missing in many cases is input from the people who would actually be using the product or operating the equipment.

When end-users are finally involved, you will tend to find a number of issues that required changes. This resulted in negative impacts to cost and schedule. In another case, you and your team members had made changes to a product as part of an upgrade that involved removing some capability that the customer said wasn't used. After the change, the end-users inform us that they are using the product in a way that neither we nor the customer is aware and they consider the now-missing capability very valuable. Needless to say, this results in unnecessary cost and a negative impact on the ability of our end users to do their job. Always involve end users in your project early on and increase the probability of avoiding many of these problems.

Include a Traceability Matrix in Your Requirements Documentation

It is often very handy to be able to trace a requirement back to its origin, especially on a complex project or on one where requirements come from multiple sources. Sometimes the project team will run into problems trying to meet a specific requirement and it is helpful to be able to find out exactly where the requirement originated, to get clarification or modification of the requirement.

Always be able to trace each project requirement back to its source and you may be able to avoid unnecessary or wasteful requirements.

Obtain Customer Agreement (Buy In) for Each Project Requirement

Sometimes requirements are not well written and the language or wording leaves the meaning of the requirement open to interpretation. For instance, a requirement that states that a specific part shall be "as light as possible" is open to interpretation. "Light as possible" may have one meaning to the mechanical engineer who designed the part, and another meaning to the customer logistics engineer who is responsible for accepting the part. The end user who has to carry the part in the field may have a third interpretation of the phrase "light as possible."

The problem arises when it is time for the customer to accept the product, and a disagreement develops as to whether or not the part meets the requirement and can be accepted by the customer. Should this occur, it creates a situation where the contractor and customer are in disagreement as to whether the part is acceptable and could result in rejection of the part and costly rework, not to mention a damaged customer relationship. Always take the time to meet with the customer early in the project and review requirements line by line.

This ensures that everyone has the same understanding of each requirement, of what it includes (and does not include), and of exactly what will be delivered.

Document Methods of Requirements Verification and Be Sure That All Parties Are in Agreement as to How Each Requirement Will be Verified

As the project nears its completion, there will be some form of acceptance testing or requirements verification conducted with the customer. This is the point where the customer can ensure that the project has successfully produced everything that was agreed upon.

Typically, compliance with each requirement is verified through inspection, demonstration, testing, or analysis. Whichever method is chosen for a given requirement should be documented early in the project, with enough detail, that the project team has a clear understanding of what will be needed to demonstrate compliance and what constitutes non-compliance. This effort is sometimes neglected as it does require planning time early in the project. The risk created by neglecting this step in planning is that it may not be possible to demonstrate compliance, to the customer's satisfaction, with one or more requirements. This could result in the project deliverables being rejected, or in costly re-work to modify deliverables. Another likely outcome is a delay in payment for project deliverables and damage to the customer relationship. Always take the time early in the project to be sure there is complete agreement on the methods of verification for each requirement.

Provide Regular Feedback to Your Team Members

People want and need regular feedback as to their performance, so they know where they are doing well and where they need to improve. As a project manager, you probably won't be involved in the annual performance review process regarding the members of your project team. However, that doesn't release you from the obligation to provide performance feedback on a regular basis. You should meet with each team member periodically (quarterly or more often, depending on the length of the project) to provide feedback on what that person is doing well and where improvement is needed. Don't let performance issues go unaddressed (or let good performance go unrecognized), communicate with individual team members often, and build a stronger, higher performing team.

Create a Culture Where Your Team is Encouraged to Provide Regular Feedback to You

Just as your team wants and needs regular feedback to maintain and improve their level of commitment and performance, so do you. You should welcome and encourage feedback from members of your team (and anyone else with whom you interact, for that matter) and utilize that feedback in a way that helps you to improve your performance. You should also remember to welcome positive as well as negative feedback with equal enthusiasm.

Positive and negative feedback are equally valuable to your goal of improving your performance as well as improving the performance of the team. In order to create an environment where team members are comfortable in approaching you with feedback, you need to have established trust and safety within your team. They need to know there is no risk in giving you feedback, especially if that feedback deals with an area that needs improvement.

Trust and safety are established over time through behavior that reinforces those ideas (i.e., no screaming, public ridicule of ideas, personal attacks, attacks on people not present, etc.). It requires not only that the project manager behave in a way that is consistent with those ideas, but that he enforce appropriate behavior with all members of the team as well. Create an environment that encourages feedback from your team and enjoy the benefits of continuous improvement and higher performance for both yourself and your team.

Co-locate Your Team to the Greatest Extent Possible

Co-location of your project team (physically locating them all in the same general area) can be very beneficial to your project and can significantly increase your probability of success, provided you understand why it works and proceed accordingly. One of the strongest arguments for co-locating your team is the potential for shared information between team members and encouragement of osmotic communication. Information sharing between individuals as well as through the use of information radiators encourages cross-functionality and makes the team stronger. This information sharing works best when the team is co-located.

Osmotic communication can be described as "positive eavesdropping" where one team member can overhear other team members discussing a problem and make a positive contribution to the resolution of that problem. Osmotic communication can only occur if the team members are located close enough to one another to overhear conversations. The most important rule for co-location is that everyone must be working on the same project. When people who are working on various unrelated projects are co-located, a noisy, distracting environment often results. This kind of environment can make it difficult for people to concentrate or focus and can often lead to reduced productivity, lower morale and negative results. Only co-locate individuals who are working on the same project.

Avoid Fractional Assignment of Your Team Members Whenever Possible

Fractional assignment is a term that comes from the world of agile methodologies and refers to individuals supporting several projects at the same time. While this is a reality in many organizations, this unfortunate practice is minimally productive and should be avoided whenever possible.

During the eighties and nineties a management belief developed that pushed the idea of multitasking and people who professed to be good at multi-tasking were seen as very valuable and highly productive. The reality is that people are not naturally wired to multitask, and most people (regardless of what they may think) don't do it well particularly if their work is highly complex or technical.

When people shift between tasks, it takes a certain amount of time for them to get back up to a productive level in the task at hand. The more switching between tasks that takes place, the more time is wasted in getting back up to speed. Switching between multiple tasks can quickly add up to a significant amount of lost time. Do all you can do to avoid fractional assignment of individuals on your team.

Don't Commit to a Project that, Because of an Unrealistic Schedule or Budget, is Doomed to Fail

Let's go through this example, a study conducted by certain group. The goal of the study was to identify communications issues that had a negative impact on project success, and the result was the identification of five items.

One of those items was defined as "fact-free planning" where plans were made without any regard for the facts. This approach is commonly seen in the creation of project schedules and budgets.

It is not uncommon for management to state that a specific project will be completed by a certain date and for a certain amount of money, without any input at all from the people who will manage the project and do the work. It is also not uncommon for project managers to accept these conditions without comment other than to say things like "we'll get it done" or "we'll do whatever it takes."

As a progressive and open-mined project manager, you should never accept these conditions, as they almost certainly guarantee the project will come in late and over budget, if it even finishes at all. It also guarantees that you and your team will work many long hours and weekends that will be full of stress. Last, but not least, you are likely to lose several people due to the unpleasant working conditions, and the ones that leave are likely to be your higher-performing people.

Instead of accepting the conditions when faced with an unrealistic proposal, you should request time to evaluate the scope with your team and return with a more realistic plan. The realistic plan may have a reduced scope, a longer schedule, or a larger budget. It might also look exactly like the original proposal. The point is that whatever you commit to should have been well thought out with input from the project team and it should be as accurate as possible. Don't commit to unrealistic plans and enjoy a happier and more successful project management experience.

Make Use of Information Radiators

"Information radiator" is a term that comes from the agile world that refers to graphic displays of information posted on walls, usually in the common work area of the project team. The intent is to conveniently provide as much information, as possible, to the project team, as well as to other interested parties. A common example in traditional project management is the posting of the project schedule in the form of a Gantt chart.

Another information radiator is the graphic form of the WBS that is color coded showing work in progress, work completed, work running behind schedule, and work not yet started. This one graphic provides a snapshot of the project's progress to anyone who is interested.

Your team doesn't need to be co-located in a common work area to use information radiators, although that would work best. If the team doesn't have a common work area, post the radiators in areas commonly used by the team.

Remember: The idea is to be as transparent and to provide as much information as possible to the team as well as other interested parties, and information radiators provide an easy way to do this.

Be Present During Conversations

Have you ever walked into the office of your boss or colleague to discuss an issue only to have them talk to you over their computer as they continue to type or check email? Have you ever been having a conversation with someone who continually checks their messages, texts, or worst of all, answers a call in the middle of your conversation? This kind of behavior is not only rude and disrespectful, but more importantly, it indicates that the person behaving this way is not really engaged in the conversation and is not going to be able to contribute fully to the subject being discussed. As an open-minded project manager, you should never engage in this behavior, nor should you tolerate it from others

When someone comes to your office for a discussion, come out from behind your desk and interact at the table (if you have one), or fold down the screen of your laptop or move so that you cannot see your monitor and give your visitor your full attention. Never have your cell phone out or respond to a call or check a message during a conversation. There is almost nothing that can come in over the phone that can't wait until you are finished. If you really are working on something urgent or have no time at the moment, ask your visitor to come back at a later time when you can devote your full attention to the conversation. Do this and you'll not only have better, more productive conversations, but you will build stronger relationships with those with whom you interact.

Apply the Concept of Caves and Commons to Your Co-located Team

If you are able to co-locate your team (being sure that the co-located people are all working on the same project), and enjoy the many benefits of co-location, you will notice the need for people to have private, quiet workspace from time to time. This need could arise when team members are doing complex design or analysis work, making phone calls to vendors or customers, or for a number of other reasons.

In the agile world the term "caves and commons" is used to describe a workspace configuration where the team is co-located and working in a common area but a conference room and a number of individual offices are provided nearby to be used as necessary by team members. By designing the workspace this way you can take advantage of the common work area by optimizing the effectiveness of information radiators and encouraging osmotic communication. In addition, you are also providing private space for team members to use as needed. Apply the caves and commons approach when configuring the team's workspace and enjoy the best of both worlds.

Work to Consistently Use an Inquiry Rather Than an Advocacy Communication Model

As project managers, we spend a great deal of time communicating, in one form or another, with other people with a significant portion of that communication consisting of face to face communication or conversations. There are two models of communication used by most of us as we converse: the advocacy model and the inquiry model.

The advocacy model is the model used by most of us most of the time and is, unfortunately, the less productive of the two. In the advocacy model each person "advocates" a position, usually arguing why their position is best and why the other position is less desirable. The advocacy model produces a winner and a loser, encourages people to hide weaknesses in their position, and is unlikely to result in real commitment to the decision by the losing party.

This approach is also less likely to result in the best decision for the project or the organization.

The inquiry model is a question-based approach (What makes you say that? Can you explain that to me a little more?) where each party attempts to understand the other party's position. The inquiry model more often results in a collaborative decision that can be fully supported by both parties as both had a hand in its creation. Decisions reached in this way are also more likely to have their weaknesses discussed and addressed and are more likely to result in better decisions for the project and the organization. Work to develop the habit of using an inquiry communication model in all your conversations and enjoy better and more productive communications with those with whom you interact.

When Creating Project Management Policies and Procedures for Your Organization, Build in Flexibility by Including an "Opt Out" Option

One of the more challenging aspects of implementing a formal project management approach in an organization is getting people to buy into new processes and procedures, and to actually use them. This can be particularly challenging when it involves individuals with a great deal of experience (especially if most of that experience is with a single employer), and no formal project management training or certification.

One way to approach this challenge in an organization is to allow project managers to "opt out" of certain parts of certain procedures under certain conditions. The intent is to ensure that they are using the procedures but to give them the flexibility or autonomy to not do things that they do not feel have add value to their project.

Use Only Those Project Management Tools and Techniques That Work and Add Value

Sometimes organizations will make a commitment to developing formal project management policies and procedures only to have employees complain and ignore them. Occasionally people will even expend a surprising amount of energy to find workarounds to the new policies and procedures. The cause of this behavior is often the result of management implementing project management procedures that are not necessary for a particular organization and are viewed by employees as adding work, but no value.

Few organizations have the resources or the need to implement everything described in the PMBOK, however a solid understanding of those project management principles is necessary to know which are appropriate and which can be ignored. After careful consideration, implement only tools and techniques that are determined to add value to your organization.

Also try to refrain from using templates or procedures taken from other organizations (use them for ideas only); try to develop procedures that are specific to your organization. This is a case where it is often better to reinvent the wheel, as the wheel designed specifically for your organization is likely to be more readily accepted and work much better. Finally, take the time to educate employees as to the purpose of each procedure and the issue it is intended to address, as well as how the procedure is likely to make their work easier and more successful.

Seek to Influence Rather Than to Persuade

As a project manager you are in a position where communication takes up a significant part of your workday. Much of this communication involves efforts to get others to do something for you, those others being your project team, functional managers, your management, or a variety of other people. It is always better to influence those individuals into a particular course of action, rather than to persuade them.

To influence someone to action means to have them not only agree with a particular idea, but to actually believe in the idea and to want to take action.

This is much more likely to produce commitment to action, which should always be the goal. Persuasion, on the other hand, will often produce compliance rather than commitment. This may get the job done, but not at the level that an engaged, committed person will achieve.

Make a deliberate effort to influence rather than to persuade. Use an inquiry rather than an advocacy communication model, whenever possible. Involve the other person in the decision and the development of the idea to the greatest extent possible; create a knowledge worker.

Be transparent and present. Always fully engage the other person in all your communication efforts.

Use the Ten Knowledge Areas as a Starting Point for Your Project Management Plan

It a wise move to us the ten PMBOK knowledge as the outline for your plan in creating a first time project management plan.

By setting up the project management plan in this way, it forces you to consider each of the knowledge areas. This process will ensure that you have the opportunity to think about everything that your project will involve. Once you have this outline you can go through each area and include items that will add value and make sense for your organization, and ignore the others. Once you have items in place, you can go about writing the description of how each item should be addressed.

If this plan is to be used as a template for other project managers at your organization, be sure to allow them the flexibility of not adhering to every item if they don't feel the item adds value to their project. Of course, they must document their reasoning. Base your project management plan on the ten knowledge areas and you will have a strong project management plan that will help to increase the probability of success on your project.

Work to Build a Very Strong Relationship with Your Customer from the Very Beginning of the Project

The ability to develop strong relationships goes back to the people skills that you possess, and your willingness to develop those skills. In addition, you have to actively and intentionally develop strong relationships with the people with whom you interact, especially your customers. There are going to be times on every project when things are not going well. Having a strong relationship with your customer will make them more willing to be understanding and to help you work through difficulties, rather than to be adversarial and to cause you problems. A strong customer relationship will also allow them to help you with political problems within your own organization, when those situations threaten the success of your project (use this particular help as little as possible and with great caution). Develop a good relationship with your customer and enjoy a happier, more successful project management experience.

Work to Build a Strong Relationship with Your Vendors from the Very Beginning of the Project

Just as having a strong relationship with your customer is important to the success of your project (not to mention to your happiness), having a strong relationship with key vendors is also critical to project success and project manager happiness. One of the common vendor issues experienced by project managers is the late delivery of items that are critical to the project. This can happen for a number of reasons, but a common one is that your order with the vendor is relatively small compared to larger orders going to other customers.

When vendor resources are limited, they are likely to be focused on the order from the bigger customer rather than on yours, delaying delivery of your parts.

There will also be times when you receive vendor items that are incorrect or need to be reworked. You may also experience problems integrating vendor items into your system and require technical help from the vendor.

All of these issues are common occurrences during the course of most projects and the better your relationship is with your key vendors the easier, quicker, cheaper, and less painful it will be to resolve issues. Take the time to get to know your key vendors, visit their facilities, develop relationships, and you will have fewer vendor issues and the ones you do have will be much more easily resolved.

Ensure That Your Team Understands the "WHY" Behind Your Project Management Policies and Procedures

When implementing project management processes and procedures, it can be very beneficial to spend the time to ensure that people understand the purpose of the new approach. This is particularly important in an environment where people have had little exposure to formal project management practices.

Take the time to educate your team (and others impacted by the procedures) as to what the new procedure is intended to accomplish and how. In addition to increasing the probability of project success, it will make their work easier and their project experience more enjoyable. This education can take the form of formal training sessions, but the project manager should also always be looking for opportunities to educate during the many casual discussions that occur throughout the typical workday. Also point out that the intent is continuous improvement and that if the procedure is not working as planned, everyone is encouraged to suggest modifications for improvement.

People resist change and formal processes for a variety of reasons. In general, the more you can help your team understand the purpose and intent of the new process or procedure, the easier and more quickly this resistance can be overcome.

Expect and be Willing to Adjust Your Project Management Plan as Your Project Unfold

Traditional project management, while not embracing change in quite the same way that agile methodologies do, works to plan for controlled change and attempts to eliminate uncontrolled change.

We create an integrated change control process as part of our project management plan specifically for the purpose of dealing with anticipated changes. The problem arises sometimes when a project manager is unwilling to adjust a plan to accommodate changing project realities. The approach in traditional project management is to plan as much of the project detail as possible and thus minimize the number of problems and have a more smoothly running project in the future. The tendency sometimes is to stick to a planned schedule or planned budget even when it becomes clear that the plans are no longer valid.

We need to remember as project managers, that our plans are just estimates of how we want things to progress and as we move through the project and learn more we must be willing to adjust plans as necessary based on new information. Remember that a plan that is no longer valid is no longer a useful project management tool. Plans that are no longer valid can also act to demoralize the team as the work that went into planning can be interpreted as wasted time producing documents that have no value. Take the time to keep your project management plan and all project documents current so that they can be used as intended and help optimize the probability of success of your project.

Publicly Recognize and Celebrate Desired Behavior from Your Team Members

As a professional and progressive project manager, you should make a deliberate effort to identify and publically recognize desirable behavior displayed by individuals on your team. By publicly recognizing this behavior, you are encouraging more of the same and also showing others what kind of behavior is desirable. In addition, you are building the kind of healthy workplace culture that will help you to develop and maintain a high performing team.

A project manager who makes it a point to find one good thing to acknowledge a team member at each team meeting and always begins the meeting with that public recognition, not only do this support the creation of a healthy work environment and encourage desirable behavior but it also help you as a project manager to focus on the good things that people on your team are doing. This, in turn, helps you with your own personal motivation.

One thing to remember when developing this practice is that the recognition should always be authentic and the recognized behavior significant and non-trivial. If the recognition becomes inauthentic it will be noticed immediately, and not only will it not achieve the positive results for which you are looking, but may actually have a negative effect on the behavior of the team.

Don't Tolerate Abusive Behavior on the Part of Your Customer

The point here is that the customer is not always right, especially when it concerns abusive behavior directed at you or a member of your team.

There is never any justification for abusive behavior in a business setting, and it should not be tolerated.

As a project manager you have a responsibility to ensure that neither you nor any members of your team are subject to abusive behavior from your customer (or from anyone in the workplace for that matter). Anyone can lose his or her temper from time to time and behave in an unprofessional manner, but consistent repeated abusive behavior must be addressed and stopped.

Confronting the behavior in private with the offender is better, however sometimes the behavior must be addressed in public. When confronting this behavior in public, care must be taken to avoid escalating the bad behavior or being drawn into an unprofessional exchange. Dealing with abusive behavior from a customer or someone above you in management is always challenging and must be approached with caution, but it is something that must be done. You can always seek help from your boss, a mentor, or someone in higher level than you, but the bottom line is that abusive behavior in the workplace should not be tolerated.

Don't Hide or Delay in Reporting Bad News to Your Customer

No one likes to be surprised by bad news. In the case of your customer or senior management, surprises of this nature are more likely to cause an unpleasant response. Customers and bosses, like most of us, usually have someone to whom they report and who is holding them accountable for the work that you are doing. Surprising your boss or customer with bad news often forces them into the same position with their superiors, which is unlikely to do good things for you or your career.

Always report bad news accurately with adequate detail and in a timely manner. Having said that let me go on to the more advanced part of this topic.

It is very important to know when to report bad news and in what level of detail to specific customers and senior managers. This "skill" requires a fair amount of emotional intelligence and also requires that you have taken the time to build a strong relationship with these individuals. Some people in positions of authority take hearing about a problem on a project as a personal challenge and feel required to personally take over and solve the problem. This kind of reaction often makes things worse and causes additional problems such as de-motivating the team or forcing a less than optimal solution.

As a project manager, you must have the emotional intelligence to anticipate the likely reaction to the news you are delivering and a good feel for when it is time to deliver the news. In addition, you must also have taken the time to build a strong relationship with your boss or customer so that you can use this relationship to help guide the reaction to a productive outcome. Never delay the reporting of bad news, but be smart about how and when you do it.

Encourage Your Customer to Review Your Project Management Plan

This is something that is easy to do and will produce a number of great benefits. Before I go further, though, I want to point out that I'm not suggesting that you give your customer approval authority over your plan, but only that you encourage your customer to review your plan. The first benefit is that it will instill confidence as your customer will likely be impressed with the thoroughness of your plan. The fact that you even have a written plan to guide the management of his project is going to be very impressive, as it's unlikely that he sees many project management plans given the number of project managers who don't understand the value of creating a written plan.

Another benefit will become apparent as you begin to respond to the many customer change requests that are likely to occur over the course of your project. By having a documented change control process, which your customer has already reviewed, it becomes much easier to respond to customer requested out of scope changes. We all know that an out of scope change request should result in a request for additional funding and a possible adjustment to the schedule. We also know that you can only give that response to your customer so many times before the relationship begins to strain. Having a documented change control process that the customer is familiar with allows the project manager more flexibility in resisting out of scope (and unfunded) change requests and reduces the likelihood of a strained customer relationship.

Limit Yourself and Agree to Manage No More Than Two Projects at One Time

This may sound unrealistic to many of you given the typical conditions in many organizations, but the reality is that in order to be effective as a project manager you need time to focus on your project. Managing multiple projects greatly reduces your likelihood of success.

As project managers, we are responsible for planning out a project and then guiding the execution of that project to a successful conclusion. Being responsible for multiple projects makes it very unlikely that you will have the time to plan and manage projects adequately, thus setting the stage for a very high-stress and unpleasant experience which is likely to end in failure. If you are forced to commit to multiple projects, employ a Deputy PM, project coordinator or expeditor, who can share the workload. The Deputy and coordinator positions can be staffed by more junior personnel who can use the experience to be mentored and to eventually become project managers. Limit the number of projects that you agree to manage concurrently and maximize your probability of success; this is good for you, your team and the organization.

Gain a Full Understanding of the Skill Sets Required for Your Project as Early as Possible

This is another one of those tips that seems very obvious but is often neglected at the beginning of a project. Like many of the techniques in this book, the information seems obvious when you read it, but is only valuable when put into practice, and it can't be put into practice if you are not first aware of it.

There seems to be a general resistance by management to allow adequate time for planning at the start of a project. There are many reasons for this resistance, but one of the risks in not allowing adequate time to plan is that you may not understand exactly what skills are required by the team to complete the project.

Always take the time to thoroughly review and understand requirements so that you fully understand the skills required of the team to successfully complete the project work.

Take the Time to Create a Human Resource Management plan within Your Project Management Plan

This is an area that is often neglected by busy project managers, many of whom don't see the risk in ignoring this part of the project plan. The process of writing out this plan will help you identify necessary skill sets and numbers of people that you will need on the project. It will also force you to consider when people are needed and how you will work them into and out of the project in a controlled manner. In addition, it will help you identify and obtain necessary training for team members in advance, rather than discovering the need in the middle of the project.

Often, one of the first questions a functional manager will ask is "When do you need him?" or "How long will you need her?" Remember that functional managers typically provide people for a number of projects simultaneously and he or she is asking these questions of each project manager. Another thing to keep in mind is that it is likely that the schedules on at least some of these other projects are slipping, making the functional manager's job more difficult.

Being able to show (or better yet involve) a functional manager in the creation of a detailed human resources management plan will go a long way in helping you get the people you want, not just the ones that are available, when you need them.

Ensure that Issues Are Handled at the Lowest Level Possible

Part of developing a positive work environment for your team is instilling the idea that each team member has the authority and responsibility to make decisions and take action regarding the success of the project. When issues arise, team members must feel empowered to take action and address the issue. An open-minded project manager does this by creating an environment of trust and safety, and sets the expectation of this desired behavior within the team.

Empowered team members will make mistakes from time to time. It is crucial that mistakes are handled as the learning experiences that they are without assigning blame or criticizing those involved. Issues should be escalated to the PM only after the team has attempted to resolve the issue without success and requests the PM's involvement.

By the same token, the issue should not escalate beyond the project manager until a reasonable effort has been made at the PM level and a determination has been made that resources beyond those possessed by the PM are required. The decision to escalate should be made by the people doing the escalating and never by those to whom the issue is being escalated. The escalation process should be described in the project management plan and be understood by everyone on the project team.

Work to Recognize and Avoid "Group Think" on Your Project

Groupthink is a common phenomenon seen in organizations or projects where there is an unhealthy workplace culture. When a leader is not receptive to ideas from subordinates and tends to reject ideas out of hand, or publicly ridicule those offering ideas that differ from theirs, the environment is set for the development of groupthink. In this unsafe environment, team members tend to focus on compromise and consensus with the goal of avoiding conflict. This approach comes with the price of minimizing critical thinking, less analysis of ideas, and often results in suboptimal decisions. In addition, this behavior demoralizes team members and causes the highest performers to shut down and behave with compliance, rather than engagement.

When groupthink occurs, the team tends to support whatever idea the leader supports without offering critical evaluation or alternatives. This tends to minimize the value and contributions of the team. The progressive project manager recognizes this danger and creates an environment of trust where ideas are openly offered and debated. The team now works in a productive environment with the goal of making the best decisions and optimizing performance. Encourage honest debate in a safe environment and avoid groupthink on your project.

Never Schedule a Full Time Individual for More than 80% on Your Project

This is a mistake that is commonly made by project managers. A reality in the workplace is that people do not do productive work for 100% of the time that they are present at the office. This isn't necessarily good or bad, it's just reality. People are required to attend staff meetings and other events that are not related to the project to which they are assigned. There are also phone calls and emails from those outside the project that must be addressed. In addition, there are requests for help and advice on work-related issues that require time, especially from those who are more senior and knowledgeable. Finally, human always have the tendency of taking time to talk with colleagues about their weekend, the local sports team, their children, and the rest of life.

When creating a project schedule and assigning resources to activities, the project manager who schedules full time individuals at 100% (i.e. 40 hours per week) is setting himself up for failure. The enlightened project manager will take the realities of the workplace into account when creating his project schedule and assigning resources and won't schedule anyone (including himself) for more than 80% (32 hours per week) on the project. Follow this tip and be able to more easily create and maintain a sustainable work pace that will improve the morale and performance of your project team.

Be Conscious of Span of Control on Large Projects and Utilize Your Staff Effectively

Project managers often make the mistake of being too engaged in the work of the project with the result being they are less effective as a project manager.

The enlightened project manager learns to trust his senior

subordinates and allows them to run their areas of the project. Building trust requires that people be allowed and encouraged to make decisions. When a mistake is made (as will happen from time to time), the mistake is treated as a learning opportunity, and the individual is encouraged to learn from his mistake and move forward.

Military leaders who command hundreds of thousands of troops do so by directly commanding a handful of senior officers, who in turn direct a handful of officers immediately below them, and so on until all the troops are under command. By trusting those officers immediately below them in the chain of command, the leader can effectively control hundreds of thousands of troops by directing a handful of people.

The enlightened project manager can utilize the same principle by directing the lead people on the project team and trusting that the work will get done properly throughout the project. By doing so, the project manager is free to focus on higher level tasks that require his attention, while allowing the work of the project to progress. In addition, by allowing the project team leads to work, he is building trust and improving moral and performance throughout the project team.

When Using Virtual Teams Try to Get Everyone Together for a Face to Face Meeting at Least Once Early in the Project

There is something about the way that human beings are wired that makes it beneficial for us to meet the people with whom we interact.

If it is at all possible, try to arrange to bring your entire team together early in the project for a face to face meeting. The kickoff meeting is an ideal event in which to accomplish this, and you should try to allocate a budget to do so.

Having the entire team meet face to face will go a long way in helping to establish and build trust within the team, something that is critical for high performance and project success.

In addition, it is very likely that valuable project-related information will be exchanged in face-to-face meetings as teammates meet each other and socialize. This information would likely have remained undiscovered or would have become known much later in the project were it forced to depend on emails or phone conversations. Finally, face-to-face meetings are more likely to result in team members forming professional relationships. These relationships will prove beneficial later, as the team addresses the many technical challenges that commonly occur during all projects. Arrange to bring the entire team together once in the beginning of the project, and reap the benefits throughout the life of your project.

Take the Time to Determine a Stakeholder's Preferred Method of Communication and Use That Method With That Stakeholder Whenever Possible

In our current age of high-tech and ever-changing communication choices, people are developing preferred methods of communication. An open-minded project manager will take the time to learn a stakeholder's preferred method and utilize that method when communicating with that particular stakeholder.

In a business setting, some people view phone calls as an intrusive, unnecessary drain on their time and therefore don't answer the phone, as they work choosing to respond to voicemail at a later time. The problem is that there is never a good "later time" and the response can be greatly delayed or never received at all. That same individual may view a text message as very convenient and efficient and tends to respond to them immediately. There is no point trying to understand the rationale or attempting to change the behavior, but only to determine the preferred method and use it when communicating with that particular stakeholder. Determine and use a stakeholder's preferred method of communication and enjoy improved, and more effective, communication.

Use Rolling Wave Planning to Optimize the Use of Limited Resources

We often use rolling wave planning during the planning process on traditionally managed projects. Rolling wave planning refers to the iterative practice of planning or estimating tasks that are relatively far out on the schedule only to the level that is supported by the information you have at the time. As you get closer to the planned task and more information becomes available, the tasks are fleshed out until they are planned to sufficient detail.

For instance, if you know that system testing will be required fourteen months into your project; you might build a number of testing events into the schedule at about that time. Since the hardware is not currently designed, there are no test plans or test procedures available to define the testing events in detail. As the design evolves and test plans and procedures are developed, plans for test events can be fleshed out until they contain sufficient detail.

In the agile world, the tendency is to plan only near-term work in detail, and not spend a lot of time planning events that are further out. The reasoning is that the same people that have to do the work are required to help plan the work. Their time is better spent doing actual work rather than planning details of work that is far out on the schedule and likely to change. We can selectively apply this concept in the traditional world by consciously thinking about tasks that will occur far into the future during the planning process, and deliberately planning those tasks only to the level of detail that makes sense and adds value. This usually cannot be done across the board on traditionally managed projects, but can be applied to specific areas to help optimize the use of scarce resources.

Work to Help Your Boss Reach a Level of Conscious Incompetence

When people learn a new skill, they generally go through four levels, or stages, of competence. The highest level is "unconscious competence," where the skill level is such that the skill can be performed without thinking about it. A good example (at least for most people) is driving a car. The next level down is "conscious competence," where the skill is still performed very well but with some conscious effort. An illustration may be the way a young driver might operate an automobile. The lowest level is "unconscious incompetence," where the knowledge regarding the skill is so low that an individual doesn't know how much he doesn't know, or even that he needs help. Unfortunately, this level is occupied by many senior managers when it comes to the subject of project management.

The level with which we are concerned is the third level down, "conscious incompetence". At this level, an individual possesses a certain level of skill but is aware that he is not performing at a satisfactory level and needs to learn more in order to master the skill. As a project manager you have a responsibility to help your organization to conduct its project work in such a way as to make the organization as successful as possible. Often, this involves educating management as to the benefits of formal project management and helping them to understand what tools and training they need to provide to the project teams. It also includes helping decision makers at your organization understand, develop, and implement policies and procedures required to support successful project management. Help your boss understand the need for formal project management and enjoy more success and happiness for the organization, yourself, and your team.

Embrace the Idea of "Minimally Sufficient"

This is another concept that comes to us from the world of agile methodologies. The basic idea is to do only what is necessary to accomplish whatever you are trying to accomplish, and no more. In the agile world, this concept is most visibly applied to documentation; however, we can apply it to many aspects of traditionally managed projects, not just documentation.

As a project manager, be vigilant from the early planning stages about the work your team is required to do to complete the project. Be thorough in your requirements analysis. Is each requirement necessary? Are any requirements excessive? Does all required documentation add value or can some be reduced and still retain value? Often the customer or those in management require things without a full understanding of the value or impact of the things they require. It's not intentional on their part, but in the busy workplace, they sometimes lose track of these things and it is up to the project manager to be a last line of defense.

Look also to your processes and procedures. Are you holding too many meetings? Do your meetings involve only the people that are really required and are they efficient and effective? Are project reviews excessive and do they add value? Are there better ways to gather and disseminate information? By asking these questions, you can be deliberate in your goal of reducing wasted effort and maximizing the productivity of your team.

Work to Reduce the Creation and Hoarding of Tacit Knowledge

Tacit knowledge is knowledge that is held and used by individuals but is not generally available to the team. This is also sometimes described as "tribal knowledge." Tacit or tribal knowledge occurs in all organizations and can exist in the form of files or documents that reside on an individual computer, or in the form of a skill or information gained through experience.

The common characteristic of all forms of tacit knowledge is that it resides with a single individual and is not readily available to the team. The danger with tacit knowledge is that, should the individual leave the organization through layoff or in pursuit of other career opportunities, that knowledge is likely to be lost permanently, to the detriment of the project and the organization.

As a progressive project manager, you should strive to encourage the sharing of information within your team and encourage policies that do the same across the organization. You should also promote cross-functionality across your team members and establish mentoring opportunities between junior and more senior team members, as most people enjoy sharing what they've learned with others. As a progressive project manager, you can encourage this practice by creating a work environment that is conducive to and rewards such behavior, and by publicly recognizing and rewarding this behavior as it occurs.

Develop the Characteristics of a "Learner" Rather Than Those of a "Controller"

Let's get to a good example, Fred Kofman, in his book Conscious Business, explains that people view the world differently and the way in which people deal with those differences defines them as either a "controller" or as a "learner."[3] Kofman goes on to explain that controllers claim to have the (only) correct interpretation of any situation and know exactly what needs to be done. They tend to direct, give orders, and have very little interest in others' opinions. According to Kofman, learners tend to be humble, curious and are less certain of the exact action to take.

Learners are curious and very interested in the opinions of others in the pursuit of the best solution to a given problem.

As a progressive project manager you should work to develop the characteristics of a learner rather than those of a controller. Controller behavior more closely resembles the old school command and control approach, which is proving to be less effective with today's workers. Approaching project management as a learner is more in line with the facilitator or servant leader approach, which is likely to be more effective with the modern day team. In addition, you will be developing knowledge workers by increasing the team's involvement in the decision making process and are more likely to come up with the best solutions to project challenges. Be a learner rather than a controller and be one step closer to becoming an enlightened project manager.

Work to Develop Your Emotional Intelligence

As project managers, a very large part of what we do involves interacting with people. We interact with our team, our management, our customers and a variety of others during our typical workday.

As human beings, our behavior is driven to a large degree by our emotions, and to not have an awareness or understanding of our emotions means that we do not have full awareness or control of our behavior. Many project managers are very knowledgeable in the hard skills of project management, but are severely lacking in the soft skills (i.e. they have high IQ and low EQ). These project managers are typically seen as task-driven and "get it done" kinds of people. While they enjoy some success as project managers, their career success and the performance of their teams will be limited by their lack of EQ.

Remember that hard work and a "driven" approach cannot make up for a lack of soft skills or low emotional intelligence. Work towards becoming an enlightened project manager, take time to learn about and improve your emotional intelligence, and enjoy greater success professionally as well as personally.

Consider Using Earned Value Management (EVM) on Projects Where Appropriate

Many project managers avoid implementing earned value management (EVM) on their projects in the belief that it is too much work or is too difficult.

Projects can become very complex very quickly, and tools that provide greater visibility into the project can be of great value to the project manager. Earned value management is one of those tools.

EVM is not as difficult as many project managers believe. In fact, the values required by EVM are already being generated by the project regardless of whether or not EVM is being used. Planned Value (PV) numbers are created during cost estimating. Actual Cost (AC) is generated by normal payroll and accounting functions. Earned Value (EV) is generated as a function of tracking percent complete, a normal monitor and control activity on all projects. Applying these values to several very simple equations will provide great insight into the health and progress of the project as well as forecasting how the project is likely to finish in terms of cost and schedule based on current data. In addition, the insight provided by EVM is based on verifiable project performance data. This tends to make the information more credible when used as a part of project status reporting to management and customers. Take the time to learn and apply EVM to your projects, when appropriate, and enjoy the benefits of greater visibility into and more control of your projects.

Be Sure to Have the Appropriate People Present for All Customer Meetings and Telecoms

This is another one of those ideas that seems obvious yet is easy to overlook.

The problem here is that we all have different perspectives through which we process information, especially when we participate in meetings. I'm looking at things from a project manager's perspective. Let's put in a perspective of an engineering management me myself working as a project manager. I tend to focus on what needs to be done to successfully complete the project work. While I'm also aware of contractual issues, this is not my main area of expertise and is not where I tend to focus. The contracts person, on the other hand, is focused exactly on issues that could impact the contract and is very tuned into any changes that could adversely impact the project from the contractual perspective. The lesson here is to not be distracted by personality or resource issues, and to be sure you have the appropriate people present at all customer meetings and telecoms.

Beware of False Precision in Your Project Management Processes and Activities

Sometimes when we use various tools to create charts and graphs for project status reporting, we tend to forget exactly how we generated the base data used to create these outputs. Using spreadsheets, charts and graphs is essential to good project management; however, we need to be mindful of the origin of the numbers used as input for these tools. Entering numbers into a spreadsheet and running them through various equations does not make those numbers any more accurate or precise. Most people tend to look at numbers on a spreadsheet and conclude that the numbers correctly measure or portray whatever area that they are intended to describe. This is a common reaction to information presented in the form of charts and graphs, especially if the graphics are well done.

As a project manager, you need to be aware of the origin of all data being used in this fashion and proceed accordingly. If the original input data consisted of estimates (or rough estimates); then the output data, graphs, or charts will also represent estimates. No matter how "pretty" the output looks; it still just represents estimated data. Always be mindful of how input data was developed and avoid the mistake of assigning a false precision to project performance information.

Be Sure to Create Clearly Defined Acceptance Criteria for Project Deliverables at the Beginning of the Project

Few things are more frustrating (or unpleasant) than arriving at the end of a project only to have the customer disagree with you as to the meaning of the stated acceptance criteria and refuse to accept the project deliverables. Acceptance criteria, like requirements, should be clearly written and specific such that there can only be one interpretation as to the meaning. If two people can read the acceptance criteria for a specific deliverable and have two different interpretations as to its meaning, the acceptance criteria needs to be re-written until there is only one possible interpretation. Furthermore, all acceptance criteria should be reviewed and agreed to by the customer at the beginning of the project so that there is no doubt as to what the project team is agreeing to deliver.

When disagreement over acceptance criteria of a deliverable occurs late or at the end of a project, it can produce significant added cost to the seller. In addition, it can also result in damaged customer relationships as well as the possibility of lost future business with that customer. Always take the time to write accurate and specific acceptance criteria and obtain customer agreement at the beginning of the project. Do this consistently and avoid disappointment at the end of your projects.

Consider Determination of Percent Complete When Creating Your Activity List

This is a point that can be easily overlooked as you create your activity list and develop your project schedule. Determining percent complete is required if you are applying earned value management to your project, but it is also necessary in the day-to-day management and monitoring of your project, even if you are not applying EVM. Customers and management will often inquire as to percent complete regarding specific tasks particularly if those tasks are related to a high visibility area of the project.

One of the worst things you can do is respond to a percent complete inquiry with an answer that is obviously a guess or very rough estimate. This kind of response will do immediate and significant damage to your credibility and will greatly undermine the confidence that your customer and management have in your ability to successfully manage the project.

When creating project activities and tasks, create specific measurable items within each task or activity that can be used to define percent complete of the task. This is not difficult to do and becomes even easier if you follow the forty hour rule when developing your project schedule. Include in your WBS dictionary the percent complete determination criteria for each WBS item. Apply this tip and avoid damage to the credibility and level of trust that you've worked so hard to establish with your customer and management.

Search for the Third Solution When Resolving Conflict

When conflict arises on a project, best practices encourage confronting the problem early and working the issue until an acceptable resolution is reached. Those of us with experience in this area (which includes just about everyone with any workplace experience) know that this is sometimes more easily said than done, and it doesn't necessarily result in the best decision for the project.

It is mainly advocated that we work to find a third solution for the conflict, one that is better than either of the two positions being advocated by conflicted parties. This approach, while simple in theory, can be difficult to apply but is worth the effort as it will frequently result in the best solution possible and will repair and enhance the relationship of the conflicted parties. The process begins by getting each party to agree to find a solution that is different from either of the two being advocated; this is not a compromise, but a new solution. The next step is to have each party explain their position, uninterrupted, until the other party can repeat it back to the satisfaction of the first party. Only clarifying questions may be asked during this part of the process.

Once both positions are fully understood, the two parties can work to create a third alternative that, when reached, should have the full support of both parties and should offer the best solution to the conflict.

Be Sure to Fully Understand the Implications of All Customer Quality Requirements at the Beginning of the Project

This is, again, one of those things that sounds like common sense but is easy to miss; it's common sense but not common practice. The practical implication of this requirement causes considerable disruption to the manufacturing phase of the project.

Always take the time at the beginning of the project to fully understand the implications of customer imposed quality requirements and be happier and more successful.

Recruit Team Members Based More on Attitude and Fit into the Team than on Possession of Specific Skill Sets

A common hiring practice followed by organizations today is to focus primarily on the specific skill set believed to be required by the position for which the candidate is being recruited. The focus is often not on the personality of the individual or whether the candidate would be a good fit in the organizational culture. This is the same approach generally followed when selecting team members.

The problem with this approach is that if the individual is not a good fit in the team or organization, it is very likely the new person will soon depart. This in turn will leave the team and the organization in the same position in which they were originally in. The other part of the problem is that when someone is not a good fit within the culture or team, the new employee and team members are typically uncomfortable, less happy, and generally less productive than they could be. This situation also tends to generate personnel problems, which the project manager is forced to handle.

Remember: When recruiting team members or hiring individuals, it is much easier to train someone who is lacking in a desired technical skill than it is to correct behavior that doesn't fit into the team or workplace culture. In addition, it is generally less painful to tolerate a learning curve period as someone acquires a new skill than it is to tolerate the period of turmoil caused by someone whose personality traits negatively impact the team or organization. Focus a little more on personality and cultural fit, and a little less on obtaining an exact skill set, the next time you recruit a new team member or hire someone and see what happens.

Be Sure to Have a Well Thought Out Implementation Plan

When rolling Out a New Project Management Policy or Procedure Sometimes when a new idea or approach is implemented, the results are unsatisfactory and the new idea is scrapped. Often the issue is not that the idea was bad for the specific organization or situation, but the implementation was incorrect or ineffective. When this happens, something that might have been a good idea and very valuable to the organization is discarded as something that was tried but didn't work. Consequently, the organization loses the opportunity to benefit from a good idea.

When implementing a new project management policy or procedure, take the time to thoroughly analyze and plan an effective implementation approach with your team. By doing this, if policy or procedure doesn't work out, you are sure it was not due to the way in which it was implemented. Also, remember to involve the team and any other appropriate individuals in the planning of the implementation. By involving the team and others, you will increase the likelihood of buy-in and success, and you will also avoid the mistake of thinking that you always have the best idea and plan (which we know isn't true). Take the time to develop a well-thought-out implementation plan for your new project management policies and procedures and enjoy greater success.

Don't Just Get the Right People on the Bus; Be Sure They Are in the Right Seats

This is important at the project level as well. It is also very important to look beyond required hard skills and focus on the candidate's attitude and fit into your work culture. when recruiting a new member for your team.

However, the next step, and the point of this tip, is to be sure you are optimizing the potential of each team member by utilizing that person where he or she is strongest. You can see how this is probably not the best use of the available resource.

Get the right people on the bus and make sure they are in the right seats to ensure the highest probability of success for your projects.

Confront the Other Conflict (early and often)

Conflict between two or more people is generally productive when that conflict is restricted to policy or ideas, as it tends to encourage discussion and debate and result in a decision that is optimal for the project or the organization. Unfortunately, conflict can sometimes become personal when individuals – rather than ideas – are attacked, resulting in a destructive situation.

This kind of conflict must be addressed and resolved immediately by the project manager.

Resolving conflict of this type can be complex and challenging, and the exact approaches are beyond the scope of this book. However, the point of this tip is to realize that the project manager needs to act as soon as this situation is discovered. Many people have a natural tendency to avoid conflict, hoping that the issue will work itself out over time and remove the necessity of an uncomfortable conversation. This approach is unwise for the project manager, as unaddressed personal conflict is likely to cause damage to your team that will spread and become more severe.

One general approach to avoiding or resolving personal conflict is to establish a safe environment for the team with mutually agreed-upon rules of behavior (setting norms). Establish these rules in the beginning of the project, enforce these rules always and for everyone, and you will greatly reduce the occurrence of this type of conflict. In addition, should this type of conflict occur, it will be much easier to handle if the conflicted parties understand that their behavior is unacceptable to the group.

Be Aware of the Risks and Implications When Using Crashing or Fast Tracking for Schedule Compression

There are, unfortunately, times on many projects when the project manager is asked to compress the project schedule for one reason or another. Two common methods of schedule compression are crashing (shortening the duration of one or more tasks on the critical path) or fast tracking (taking tasks on the critical path that were originally scheduled to occur sequentially and executing them in parallel with one another). While both of these methods are valid, they come with a price of which the project manager should be aware.

Crashing is likely to produce additional costs as additional resources will likely need to be applied in order to shorten the duration of specific tasks. Fast tracking generally increases risk as there were likely valid reasons for doing the tasks serially rather than in parallel in the first place and some of those reasons are likely to be risk-related.

While schedule compression may be unavoidable in some cases, the project manager should always understand the costs and risks involved. There is a likelihood that the attempted schedule compression will result in problems that will make the actual project completion date later, rather than earlier.

Remember that the original schedule was developed when the team had time and was not stressed with pressures that are typical in the middle of the executing processes, when the request for schedule compression is likely to occur. Avoid schedule compression if possible, but if you are forced to do it, be cognizant of the costs and risks, and be sure to manage expectations with your customer and management.

Apply the Theory of Small Wins

Research has shown that achieving small successes consistently is a powerful motivator for most people. Video game makers use this knowledge when designing video games that allow players to continually move to the next level, gather power, and otherwise progress in small increments. This approach causes people to experience greater satisfaction when playing, leading to more time spent on the game and more sales for the game manufacturer.

As a project manager, you can use this knowledge to help create an environment that encourages your team to stay motivated and engaged. Arrange work, to the greatest extent possible, such that the team can accomplish small tasks relatively often and publically acknowledge these accomplishments. Encourage the team to arrange their work and daily activities to maximize the potential for small victories and acknowledge them when they do so. Use team meetings and communications to celebrate small victories and include management and the customer in acknowledging the accomplishments of the team, as appropriate.

Like many things in the soft skills area, some of the greatest positive impacts to team behavior can be accomplished through the consistent use of the small things and by awareness and attention to detail. Apply the theory of small wins on your project and enjoy the benefits of a higher performing and happier project team.

Distinguish Between Positions and Interests When Dealing with Operational Conflict

There are three types of conflict we typically face in the workplace: personal, intrapersonal, and operational. Operational conflict arises when there is something material at stake. For instance, you may believe that a particular section of software code should be written in-house, while your colleague believes the best choice is to outsource the task to a vendor with more expertise.

In Conscious Business, it is necessary to distinguish between positions and interests in order to resolve operational conflict.

A position is a specific demand that each party brings to the conflict. An interest is the underlying desire or need that supports the position. In our example, the positions are stated as what approach each party thinks is the best one to get the software written – write the code in-house or outsource the work. The interests are the same for each party: to get the software written in a way that best serves the project. In most cases, the interest is common to both parties involved in a conflict (if the two parties didn't have a common interest, they probably wouldn't be talking).

There are times when the interests of both parties are not common. For instance, your colleague may not care about the success of the project at all and only wants to outsource the work because his brother-in-law owns the software company. In either case, it is necessary to first determine the underlying interests of each party before the conflict can be resolved. By identifying the interests of each party, common ground can be discovered and used as a starting point to find a mutually acceptable resolution to the conflict.

Review the Enlightened Project Manager Booklist and Read As Many of the Books as Possible – Or at Least the Ones That Call to You

Reading one to two books about every three weeks will install you with more ideas and information that will help you progress in your managerial projects. The reading will, in turn, move you down the path towards becoming an enlightened project manager.

My goal is to hopefully expose you to something that will prove life-change. In any event, read as many of the books entailing skills in project management as possible, and you will almost certainly find something that will not only make you a better and happier project manager, but a better and happier person. Become a progressive and enlightened project manager.

CHAPTER 7

ASSEMBLING TEAM MEMBERS AND EXECUTING PROJECT PLANS

For a well successful project, a good team with well organized members is needed. This team members help execute any broken-down task to aid the project run smoothly and efficiently.

It is unlikely that there is no need for interactivity and coordination among various aspects of the project. A good, well-organized team gets the job done right. However, a selected team must be run by you and work under your authority to effectively run the project. Below are some of the measures that you need to in cooperate to achieve best results, they include:

Have the Integrity to Stand Up for Your People

There will be times in your career when you will have to make an ethical decision, where the result could have a dramatic impact on your current employment situation. In other words, you could be fired for doing the right thing.

It's an unfortunate fact of life that there are people in management or leadership positions who shouldn't be there, and occasionally you or a member of your team are going to cross paths with one of these individuals. When someone on your team is singled out for persecution by one of these individuals, you have an obligation to defend that team member (assuming you have a complete understanding of the facts and you are convinced that your team member is in the right). There are a number of ways to go about this defense (these approaches are well beyond the scope of this book), some of which will end well and some not. The point is that as a leader, you must be willing to stand up and try when that action is warranted.

Let's say for a large number of people would not risk their job to defend one of their team members. Remember that there are other jobs out there (many, many, other jobs – most of which are better than the one you currently have), but you only have one reputation and your credibility and integrity are yours. You should ensure that these qualities are the way you want them to be.

Be Open to the Idea of Team Members Telecommuting When it Makes Sense to Do So

Occasionally, there are times when it makes sense to have team members work from home and the project manager should be receptive to this idea. The typical workday is fraught with necessary interruptions and distractions and for some individuals, working remotely to focus on certain tasks, may be a very good choice.

Working from home is not the right choice for all people and is not the answer for all projects. However, where it makes sense or when requested by a team member, it should be tried out. Again in the spirit of building a positive workplace environment, this is going to help you get that high performing team. When this is tried out, expectations for both parties needs to be clearly understood, particularly regarding communications and expected work results.

In most cases, when done correctly, the arrangement will work very well for both parties and will go a long way in building trust and creating a positive work environment

Success Has Many Fathers but Failure is an Orphan – Adopt an Orphan

One of the surest ways to lose credibility with your team is to take credit for good things resulting from the team's work. The second best surefire way to lose credibility with your team is to throw team members under the bus when things are going badly. In addition to the damage your reputation will suffer with your team, you can be sure that others in the organization will notice if you consistently engage in this behavior. The result of others taking notice of this bad behavior is unlikely to do good things for your career.

Always give the team credit for the good things that happen on a project and when bad things happen (which they do on every project), always step up and take responsibility for the issue. Like it or not, you are the captain of the ship and when good things happen, it's because of the crew and when bad things happen, it's because of the captain. Always practice this philosophy and your team as well as others in the organization will notice and you will get everything that you deserve.

Be Able to Distinguish Between a Team and a Work Group and Strive to Create the Team

We hear the word "team" used frequently in the workplace to describe various groups of people thrown together to accomplish this task or that. The reality is that while these groups are frequently referred to as teams, they are in reality workgroups: a group of individuals who are working for themselves without real commitment to a team or common goal.

A team is a very powerful entity that is much stronger than any of the individuals that make up the team. Teams are intentionally built and nurtured and require trust such that team members are willing to compensate for the weaknesses of teammates and to sacrifice to amplify the strengths of others. Professional sports teams are great examples of this concept where individuals have specific talents, skills, and jobs and work together as a team to accomplish a common goal.

Unfortunately, the workplace culture that exists in many organizations is counter to good team development and tends to incentivize people to work as individuals rather than to contribute to the good of the team. As an open-minded project manager you should strive to build the environment of trust and safety that is necessary to develop and maintain a high performing team.

Be as Flexible as Possible Regarding Working Hours – Focus on Results Rather Than on the Clock

As we move from an industrial age management paradigm towards a more knowledge worker based management paradigm, we find that the idea of rigid work hours and the eight to five workday becomes less desirable. This is particularly true with the continuing development of the internet and the many mobile devices available today. Many software developers, for instance, seem to prefer to come in later in the morning and work later into the evening than the typical workday schedule defines. As a project manager, you should accommodate these flexible hours to the greatest extent possible and focus more on the quality, amount, and timeliness of work produced rather than a rigid work schedule.

One of the keys to developing a high performing team is to establish an atmosphere of mutual trust; you need to trust your team to accomplish work without constant supervision. While some work schedule rigidity is necessary to accommodate the needs of the organization, you should be as flexible and accommodating to the needs of your team as possible, in order to encourage and maintain a high performance work environment.

If the Team is Required to Work Late or Come In on a Saturday, the PM Should Always Be There With Them

There are times when team members are going to be required to come in to work on a Saturday or to stay late during the week for several days at a time.

Sometimes there are valid reasons for this which might include: preparation for an extensive program review, resolution of a technical issue that is impacting something outside the project, some customer demand or emergency, or preparation for a significant testing event.

When it becomes necessary for the team to come in during other than normal working hours, the project manager should come in as well. While the project manager may be of minimal help to the team, he or she should be present to show support and solidarity. While you may not be hands-on helping the team, you can be in your office, working and showing that you are all part of the same team. If your people have to be there then you need to be there, as well.

This behavior will go a long way in building and maintaining the kind of work environment necessary to produce a high performing team.

Acceptable Behavior is Behavior That You Accept; Choose Wisely

When we tolerate rude or disrespectful behavior from individuals, we are "accepting" that behavior, and by default are defining that behavior as "acceptable" to us. Once we do that we can expect more of the same behavior because we have indicated to the offending individual that his or her behavior is acceptable to us and we would like it to continue.

Screaming, personally attacking individuals, belittling individuals in public (or in private), and attacking individuals who are not present are all examples of unacceptable behavior that should not be tolerated. This behavior should not be tolerated from anyone, including management, customers, and project team members.

As the project manager, you are ultimately responsible for establishing and enforcing behavioral norms where that behavior impacts your team. Your team should understand the rules defining what is considered acceptable behavior and act accordingly.

Recognize Stories and Don't Allow Them to Influence Behavior

What is interesting about stories is that we all use them. Even more troubling is that we take action based on the stories that we tell ourselves, so if those stories are usually wrong what does that say about the actions that we take based on those stories? It is impossible to accurately know why someone behaves in a certain way unless that person chooses to explain his or her behavior to you. Learn to recognize a story when you tell yourself one and question your assumptions before acting on them. Remember that the story you tell yourself regarding someone else's behavior is very likely wrong and any action you take based on that story will likely be wrong as well.

Use Daily Stand-Ups

The daily stand-up meeting is another tool that comes from the agile world that can be very useful in the traditional project management world. The daily stand-up is used primarily to synchronize the project team and to reveal any impediments to work progress that need to be addressed.

We sometimes see the daily standup used in the traditional world; however, it is typically when there is some crisis to be resolved and the rules to the daily standup are either unknown or ignored, resulting in an unproductive or de-motivating daily meeting. To get great results from the daily stand-up, the following rules must be strictly observed:

1. The meeting lasts no longer than 15 minutes.

2. The meeting is conducted where there are no chairs (it really is a stand- up meeting) .

3. Each person states the following three things and only these three things:

a) What have I worked on since the last stand-up

b) What will I work on between now and the next stand-up

c) Is there anything impeding my work that needs to be addressed?

Any problems or issues uncovered during the stand-up are discussed by the concerned individuals after the stand-up ends; problems are never discussed during the stand-up

Be Clear on the Definition of Done

This is something that seems obvious, but is ignored in many cases exactly because it seems so obvious. Everyone on the team should have the same understanding of what it means when a team member says that a task is done. It doesn't matter specifically what the definition of done is for your team, only that everyone on the team has the same understanding of what done means. Done could mean that something is complete, fully tested, and shippable or it could mean that something works, but has not been fully tested.

The exact definition is unimportant; however, that everyone has the same understanding is critical.

Define the meaning of done with your team at the beginning of the project and help everyone save time and avoid problems.

Recognize Mistakes for the Learning Opportunities That They Are

Mistakes are a normal part of the human experience and are essential to the learning process. While we naturally seek to minimize the number of mistakes that occur, we should also accept the fact that they will happen. When a mistake does occur we should utilize the event as a learning opportunity in the spirit of continuous improvement, with a goal of avoiding the same mistake in the future.

There is a tendency of those steeped in the old industrial age approach to management to hide or cover up mistakes, believing that they or their team will be viewed as less competent for having made a mistake. The problem with that reasoning is that there is no opportunity for the team to learn from the mistake and improve future performance. In addition, the likelihood that the mistake will be repeated at some point in the future is increased.

Always treat mistakes as learning opportunities for the team by discussing the cause and effect out in the open, with the team and by developing a plan to avoid repeating the same mistake in the future. Follow this practice and the team will become stronger and higher performing as your project progresses.

Look First to Yourself to Understand the Behaviors of Your Team

If you have members of your team who are not behaving in a way that is optimizing the productivity and performance of your team, look first to yourself to explain and correct the behavior. Are you leading by example and "walking the talk"? Could team members be mirroring bad behavior that they are seeing demonstrated by you? Do you appear unenthusiastic or negative regarding the project, customer, or the organization? How do you react when a team member brings you bad news; are you a "screamer"? Do you belittle the team member publicly (or privately, for that matter)?

Remember that most people believe they are doing a good job and are trying to do what they believe to be best for the project. When their performance is not what you would like it to be, many times there is a communication problem (from your side) that can resolve the issue. Remember that yours is the only behavior over which you have total and absolute control. You should always be aware of your behavior and how your actions are perceived by those around you. Use that awareness to get the results that you desire.

CHAPTER 8

PUTTING TO AN END A PROJECT

FINAL PHASE RESPONSIBILITIES

These are the final steps that are taken when you as a project manager you are about to complete or you have completed the project given. Here are some of the final checklists to be looked into to properly end the project.

•Make sure all unfinished project activities are completed. Many project managers drop the ball at this point, assuming everything is done because most tasks are completed. Assume nothing and do a thorough review.

Sometimes people cut corners to move on to their next project or operations. Don't let this happen to you. Set up a task list of final items and review it to ensure that everything is completed and the quality of the work is satisfactory.

•Have a team meeting to evaluate the project. You may do one meeting with your team to prepare a wrap-up presentation for stakeholders. Determine how you got where you are, and what you might do differently in the future.

Review your documentation to be sure it's complete for the next project team. Include a thorough review of the budget, your resources, and barriers. Share what you learned the hard way to save the next team time and money.

•Meet with stakeholders, sponsors, and anyone else who needs to approve or sign off on the project. Make sure that everyone with final authority agrees that the project has concluded.

•Finish off all accounting procedures including paying final bills and fulfilling all contracts. Make sure all bookkeeping is up to date and all information for team members is accessible, including personal information needed for tax-related documents. Your goal is to close the books on the project before shutting off the lights.

•Make sure all documentation lands in the hands of those who will need it in the future. If you have created a new product or started a new service that the sales team will now be selling, make sure the sales force has all the information (such as product specifications, user tools, or plans for future development) they require.

•Meet with team members and thank them for their efforts. Let them know that the stakeholder, sponsors, and others are pleased with the job they have done. Also, thank vendors and others who were integral to the success of your project. Make sure everyone knows the project is indeed officially over, for better or worse.

•Reassign team members. If you own your own business and the team was made up of employees, you will need to either assign them to a new project, move them into operations resulting from the project, or have them return to doing their original jobs. Let people know what they should do next.

•Return all tools, equipment, or anything you borrowed to its rightful owner.

If you purchased equipment for the project, decide what to do with it.

Often, when people leave a project, a lot of "stuff" is left behind. You need to clean up the mess and determine what is necessary for project maintenance and standard operations, and what part of the project phase was. Can this equipment be used on future projects? On occasion, tools and equipment have been known to "grow legs" as the project winds down. Keep tabs on resources and equipment. If you do have some dispensable goods, give them away to team members.

•If the project was a success, celebrate! Sometimes, even a failed project is cause for celebration, recognition, and appreciation.

Successful and unsuccessful projects need to shut down in a similar manner; however, on projects that have failed, there are a few additional considerations:

•You may have a hard time convincing stakeholders that the project is indeed over. Many hopeless projects linger on indefinitely because one or more of the stakeholders do not want to accept that the end has come.

•You will have less celebrating and more consoling to do, since team members may feel frustrated or disappointed. You need to encourage team members to focus on how much was accomplished and what everyone learned. Do not rehash mistakes or lay blame; acknowledge that sometimes that's the way things work out.

•It may take longer to close the books, since there may be outstanding or irreconcilable bills. Set up a time frame in which to try to close the books.

•Depending on the project and the attitude of the team members, you may need to pay special attention to security issues.

A project may fail for many reasons. It is important that at some point the project failure is realized and accepted, and there is an official shutdown. This can take a long time if there are legal entanglements, but in most projects there is a need to acknowledge that, at some point, it may indeed be over, even if you believe in your heart it shouldn't be.

CONCLUSION

SUMMARY OF EMPLOYER FIDUCIARY RESPONSIBILITIES

This book of great knowledge has shown you all the qualities, techniques and tips needed to make you a great project manager. It has also highlighted all the best ways for you to getting that project management job. Even the best and prolific project managers may sometime have their projects unsuccessful but, this doesn't make them stop from taking other projects. Failures are there to be encountered. Just because you have had a project failure, it does not mean that you are not a good project manager. It means that you missed something that you won't miss the next time.

Don't panic if things go wrong, re-look to what made you fail and try to figure out what it should be done.

Project management can be one of the most exciting and rewarding jobs. You are in charge of doing something that has never been done before. Not only that, but you have to say when you will be done and how much it will cost. Embrace the challenge. Have fun with your teams. Enjoy the highs and lows.

Project management can be a challenge, but it is also some of the most fun that you can have. Now, go forth and manage any given project. You have what is needed now to execute any given task at hand.